THE GREAT LIVES SERIES

Great Lives biographies shed an exciting new light on the many dynamic men and women whose actions, visions, and dedication to an ideal have influenced the course of history. Their ambitions, dreams, successes and failures, the controversies they faced and the obstacles they overcame are the true stories behind these distinguished world leaders, explorers, and great Americans.

Other biographies in the Great Lives Series

ACKNOWLEDGMENT

A special thanks to educators Dr. Frank Moretti, Ph.D., Associate Headmaster of the Dalton School in New York City; Dr. Paul Mattingly, Ph.D., Professor of History at New York University; and Barbara Smith, M.S., Assistant Superintendent of the Los Angeles Unified School District, for their contributions to the Great Lives Series.

GREAT LIVES

MARTIN LUTHER KING, JR.
DREAMS FOR A NATION

By Louise Quayle

FAWCETT COLUMBINE
NEW YORK

For middle-school readers

A Fawcett Columbine Book
Published by Ballantine Books

Produced by
The Jeffrey Weiss Group, Inc.
96 Morton Street
New York, New York 10014

Library of Congress Catalog Card Number: 89-90900

ISBN: 0-449-90377-X

Cover design and illustration by Paul Davis

Manufactured in the United States of America

First Edition: February 1990

10 9 8 7 6 5 4 3 2 1

TABLE OF CONTENTS

Martin Luther King, Jr., the renowned American civil rights leader, delivered the most famous speech of his career on August 28, 1963. His theme that day was simple but moving: "I Have a Dream."

1

The Call

ON THURSDAY AFTERNOON, January 26, 1956, twenty-seven-year-old Dr. Martin Luther King, Jr., finished his daily duties as the pastor of Dexter Avenue Baptist Church in Montgomery, Alabama. Leaving the church, he climbed into his green Chevrolet and began the drive home through Montgomery's black neighborhood. On his way, he stopped to pick up a carload of passengers.

A month earlier, in December 1955, Montgomery's Negroes (as blacks or African Americans were then called) had begun a boycott of the city's buses. In other words, they refused to ride them. At that time state law dictated that blacks had to ride in the back of the bus, and blacks felt this was unfair. When a black woman named Rosa Parks was arrested for refusing to give up her seat to a white person, the blacks of Montgomery boycotted the buses in protest. With Martin Luther King, Jr. as their leader, blacks began to carpool as an alternative means of transportation. King was helping out with the carpool when he stopped to pick up passengers on that day in late January.

When he pulled his car away from the stop, two policemen on motorcycles followed him. King's passengers advised him to drive slowly. Carefully he crept along the city streets at twenty-five miles per hour. Surely, he thought, the policemen would stop following them if he drove within the speed limit. Everyone in the car tried to stay calm, but they feared what might happen. Some blacks involved in the boycott had already been beaten by angry whites. Recently, Montgomery's police had begun arresting carpool drivers for minor, and sometimes imaginary, violations.

The police stayed with King at every turn. At the next stop, when King cautiously pulled over to the curb, the police motorcycles pulled up beside his Chevrolet.

As the passengers began to get out of the car, one of the policemen spoke sharply to King: "Get out, King. You're under arrest for speeding, thirty miles an hour in a twenty-five-mile zone."

The young pastor could not believe his ears. How could they possibly arrest him for speeding when he had been driving so slowly? He kept his thoughts to himself, though. He knew that arguing with them might make matters worse. The police had already made up the charge on which they were arresting him; they would probably be happy to create another charge against him if given the chance. A patrol car was called to take King to jail.

King had never been arrested before, and he did not know what to expect. When the patrol car arrived, he asked his friends to call his wife, Coretta, and tell her what had happened. A wave of panic washed over him as he got into the backseat of the police car. King thought Montgomery's jail was downtown, but the car headed toward the outskirts of town. Where could the police be taking him? As the patrol car journeyed farther and farther away from the center of the city, King's fears grew.

In the South, especially in the heart of Alabama, the law did little to protect blacks. In fact, some laws, called segregation laws, often limited their freedom and discriminated against them. Such laws stated that blacks could not go to the same school with whites, that they had to use separate "colored only" rest rooms and drinking fountains, enter public places such as movie theaters and waiting rooms through separate entrances from whites, and ride in a special section in the back of buses and trains. These laws grew out of a racist attitude toward blacks. They were discriminated against solely on the basis of their skin color.

Many whites believed that blacks were inferior to whites in all respects, and that, therefore, they should not have the same rights as whites. A secret society called the Ku Klux Klan (KKK) had been organized to uphold this white "supremacy" (which also extended, it said, to other non-whites). KKK members burned blacks' homes and churches, and even hanged blacks simply for "talking back" to whites. When these hangings, or lynchings, occurred, the police often looked the other way. Seldom did a court of law convict a white person for harming a black.

As King rode in the back of the police car, he thought of the anger and hatred that the Montgomery bus boycott inspired in whites. He had lived with segregation and discrimination all his life. As a boy he had been called "nigger." As a man, he was called "boy." As the leader of the Montgomery Improvement Association (MIA), the group responsible for the boycott, he received as many as twenty-five calls a day from whites who objected to the boycott. Many of the calls threatened King's life and that of his wife, Coretta, and daughter, Yoki. Maybe this was the chance for which the callers had been waiting.

As the day grew dark, the police car headed farther away from the center of Montgomery, and King imagined what might happen. The car could be overtaken by a band of Klansmen. They would throw a rope over a tree branch and King would become one of the many black men lynched in the South. The police would say they had not been able to control the mob. King's effort to stop bus segregation in Montgomery would end before he could see any change in the unjust laws.

But no headlights followed the police car, and no mob appeared. The patrol car crossed a bridge, and King noticed a building in the distance lit with a neon sign that read MONTGOMERY CITY JAIL. He breathed a sigh of relief, realizing he would not die out there alone on the road. Still, King was ashamed that, as the leader of the boycott, he did not even know where the jail was. Others involved in boycotting Montgomery's buses had been arrested. King had been concerned for their safety, but he had not bothered to find out where the authorities took the protesters who depended on his leadership and guidance.

Jail presented King with new dangers. Even there blacks could not escape violence from whites. Some times the police beat black prisoners. As the police led him inside, King's senses were assaulted by the dingy conditions. The smell of urine and sweat filled the cells, and peeling paint and iron bars offered little comfort. Prisoners slept on cots. In the few cells where there were mattresses, they were torn and dirty. Officers took King to a cell where Montgomery's drunks and thieves were held. King, the pastor of Dexter Avenue Baptist Church, would be held with common criminals simply for speeding.

For the first time since the boycott began, King felt utterly alone. Before the arrest, he and other MIA leaders had had constant contact with one another and with Montgomery's blacks through nightly "mass meetings" in Dexter and other churches. At these meetings, protesters gathered to sing and pray. MIA leaders spoke to lift their spirits and pass along information about the car pools or the progress being made in negotiations with Montgomery's city govern- ment. In jail, King was cut off from this network of warmth and support.

As alone as he felt, King had compassion for the other people who had to endure the conditions in the jail. Even those who had violated the law shouldn't have to suffer in crowded cells with inadequate beds and exposed toilets, King reasoned. King's cellmates recognized him as the boycott leader, and they begged him to help them win release from jail. He stopped their pleas by explaining that before he could help them, he had to get himself out.

King's followers and colleagues on the outside had

not forgotten him. Many feared that the authorities might resort to violence to stop the movement's young leader. Coretta King and those who had witnessed his arrest, afraid for King's safety, quickly spread the word to other blacks in Montgomery. Another pastor in Montgomery was trying to get him released on bail. People from King's Dexter Avenue Baptist Church and members of the MIA piled into cars and drove to the jail to protest his imprisonment. They could not sit idly by while he was in custody.

Sometime that evening, a jailkeeper came to lead King out of his cell. King thought someone had posted bail for him, and was disappointed when he was merely taken for fingerprinting. A short time later he was back in the cell, his fingers stained from being pressed into an ink pad. It was getting late. He could expect no miracles now.

When the jailer came to lead him out of the cell a second time, however, King noticed that the jailer was nervous — and for good reason. So many blacks had gathered outside the jail that it looked as if a riot might break out. The building was virtually surrounded by King's supporters. Giving in to the public pressure, the jailer released King, warning him to appear for his trial on Monday.

King stepped onto the front steps of the jail, where he was greeted by the crowd. Shaken by his experience inside but fortified by the show of support from Montgomery's blacks, King led the crowd back to Montgomery, where a mass meeting was held. So many people showed up that they could not fit into the church. Other meetings followed, and by the end of the night, seven mass meetings were held all over the city. Martin Luther King, Jr.— and the Montgomery bus boycott — was still going strong.

King would not be stopped by threats from Montgomery's police, nor by the anonymous threatening calls he received at home. The day after his arrest, he worked a full day at Dexter. That night, he and Coretta had already gone to bed when the phone rang. The voice on the other end told him, "Listen, nigger, we've taken all we want from you. Before next week you'll be sorry you ever came to Montgomery." King had only recently moved to Alabama.

A few days earlier, someone had threatened to kill him. The day before, he had experienced the horror of a jail cell. Now he was afraid that not only he, but also Coretta or Yoki, would be hurt. King faced a real dilemma. As wrong as discrimination against blacks was, how could he put the lives of those he loved most in danger by continuing his activism? How could he be a strong, effective leader when these threats made him afraid for his own life? The thrill of leading thousands of blacks in the bus boycott was replaced by thoughts of the danger his actions could bring. He and other blacks were challenging racist attitudes and customs that had existed for hundreds of years; those attitudes would not disappear without a fight.

King hung up on the caller and went down to his kitchen to put on a pot of coffee. Pacing back and forth, he waited for the coffee to brew and contemplated all that was happening. King had been heartened by the show of support from the crowd upon his release from jail, but now his responsibilities frightened him. By asking black people to continue the boycott, he was leading entire families into danger.

He felt pressure from some blacks who wanted the boycott to end even though they had not achieved their goal of desegregation on the buses, and from whites who wanted the movement stopped at any cost. The boycott had lasted only a few weeks. Already he was exhausted, but King knew the struggle could go on for a long time.

Sitting at his kitchen table, the twenty-seven-year-old preacher held his head in his hands and spoke out loud to himself about his fears, admitting that he felt alone, that he could not go on. "I can't face it alone," he said.

In a sermon to the Dexter congregation a year later, King would describe the "inner voice" he heard that night. The voice told him he *could* go on to do what was right, to work for the cause of freeing America's blacks from oppression. As the voice reassured him, his doubts and fears all but disappeared. Now he truly felt "the call," the inner spirit and religious conviction that would continue to spur him on in the fight for racial equality.

At his trial on Monday, January 30, 1956, King was found guilty and paid a fine. But the Montgomery bus boycott would continue. In fact, the boycott would soon capture the attention of citizens all over the United States, and King would go on to succeed in desegregating the buses.

For the young preacher, being arrested and threatened made him realize he *did* have the strength to lead the fight against segregation and discrimination. From that point on, Martin Luther King, Jr., would be the voice and symbol of the fight for the rights of American blacks.

2

Preacher's Kid

MICHAEL KING, JR., whose name would later be changed to Martin Luther King, Jr., was born on January 15, 1929, in Atlanta, Georgia. Religion and the church were a part of Mike, Jr.'s life from his earliest days. His father, Michael King, Sr., was a Baptist minister, and his mother, Alberta Williams King, was the daughter of a prominent Atlanta minister. M.L., as friends and relatives eventually called "Little Mike," spent his early childhood in a church house on Auburn Avenue in the middle-class black section of the city. His family had a tradition of leadership in the black community, and M.L. was well aware of the long and troubled background of his black forefathers in the United States.

Many blacks were first brought to America as slaves in the eighteenth and nineteenth centuries. They were owned as property, just like a piece of furniture or a mule, and enjoyed few, if any, rights. It was even illegal to teach blacks to read or write. In 1861, when Abraham Lincoln began his term as

President, the Civil War broke out between the Northern states and the Southern states. There had been a lot of conflict between the North and the South, much of it over the issue of slavery. Northern states wanted slavery to be outlawed, while Southern states said it was their right to own slaves. Southern states formed the Confederate States of America and fought against the Northern states for the right to do as they pleased. The Civil War raged until the North finally won in 1865. During the war, in 1863, President Lincoln issued the Emancipation Proclamation, freeing the slaves. When the North won, the South was forced to abide by the new law, and the slaves there were freed.

In theory, blacks now had the same freedoms as whites. During a rebuilding period after the Civil War known as Reconstruction, there were some black congressmen and other blacks who enjoyed social and political gains. But most remained poor and did not have the same opportunities as whites. Southern legislators passed laws limiting their rights and privileges. For example, blacks had to pass literacy tests to vote, whereas whites did not. Even if blacks could read and write well, the white officials issuing the test often would not pass them.

Laws passed during the latter half of the nineteenth century limiting the rights of blacks were known as Jim Crow laws. The name came from a fictitious comedian who appeared in minstrel shows, which were popular at the time. White performers would blacken their faces with burnt cork and stage humorous skits, all of which made black people look like simple fools who spoke with heavy Southern accents and were not as smart as whites. Jim Crow laws were passed by Southern whites to ensure that blacks would remain in the same humiliating condition as the minstrels, so they would not become an influential voice, either socially or politically.

In 1896, the United States Supreme Court ruled in *Plessy v. Ferguson* that blacks and whites should have "separate but equal" facilities in public places such as schools and bathrooms. This Supreme Court decision formed the legal basis of the South's segregation laws. But as any black in the South knew, most of the time *separate* did not mean *equal*. Usually, the facilities for blacks were far below the standards of those for whites.

During the early years of the twentieth century, the struggle for the rights of blacks died out almost completely. Southern whites kept blacks from entering politics with voter registration laws and laws limiting the number of blacks who could be elected to state legislatures. In addition, at a time when the United States was still seeking to position itself as an international power, many people argued that emphasis on race issues weakened the country's position among other countries and undermined its economic strength. White supremacy, in the spirit of the Ku Klux Klan, captured the nation's sympathies, and the question of rights for blacks all but disappeared.

In this atmosphere, blacks saw the church as a social, political, and economic center. The National Baptist Convention's churches formed a network of thousands of blacks all over the country. Historically, too, the ministry was highly respected among blacks, and many black men worked to become preachers. Unlike white ministers, few black preachers could go to seminary to learn their trade, and since the days of slavery, they relied on good speaking skills, rather then education, to lead their congregations. To church members, the preacher was as much a leader of political opinion in the community as he was a moral leader.

"Daddy" King, as M.L.'s father was known to his family, was one in a long tradition of black Southern Baptist preachers. Daddy King had left his sharecropper family in 1913, at the age of fourteen. (Sharecroppers were poor farmers who were allowed to live on and work someone else's land. In return, they gave the owner a large portion of their harvest.) Lacking a formal education, King worked long and hard to become a preacher, and to develop his speaking skills. During the weeks he worked in a tire-manufacturing plant in Atlanta, and on the weekends he traveled in search of churches that needed a preacher.

Alberta Williams King, M.L.'s mother, came from a very different background. An educated woman, she had attended Spelman College, a school in Atlanta for black women, and was an able musician. Her father, Adam Daniel Williams, was a pastor who had made his church, the Ebenezer Baptist Church, one of Atlanta's most influential black churches. Adam Williams actively fought discrimination against black people, and was the first president of the Atlanta chapter of the National Association for the Advancement of Colored People (NAACP). Formed in 1908 to fight the anti-black legislation being passed at the time, the NAACP filed cases in local, state, and federal courts. The NAACP believed that protesting segregation laws in the courts — and relying on the U.S.

Constitution's guarantees of equal rights for all — would help push the political tide back in blacks' favor.

After Michael King and Alberta were married in 1926, they lived with Alberta's parents in the Ebenezer church house on Auburn Avenue, in Atlanta's middle-class black section. In 1932, shortly after Adam Williams's death, Michael became Ebenezer's pastor. He had achieved his goal of becoming the pastor of a major church.

The 1930s were a time of great financial hardship in the United States. In 1929, prices on the stock market had crashed to new lows, causing economic failure all over the United States and the world and ushering in an era known as the Great Depression. By 1932, 12 million people in the United States were unemployed. The Depression was especially hard for blacks, who, even in prosperous times, made less money and had fewer advantages than whites. In Atlanta, where the Kings lived, 65 percent of black people received assistance from the government.

The economic conditions of the time were taking their toll on the Ebenezer church, as everywhere else. But even during this trying period, Michael King was able to expand the role of his church. By the time he had finished his first year as Ebenezer's pastor, he had become the highest-paid minister in Atlanta.

By now his family had grown. He and Alberta had a daughter, Christine, and just before the Depression hit, in 1929, Michael, Jr., was born. Another son, Alfred Daniel, who was called A.D., was born seventeen months after M.L. Daddy King did not want his children to suffer the same financial or emotional hardships he had. He bitterly remembered that his drunken father had beaten him. He also remembered the smell of the farm on his clothes, and knew the humiliation of being called "nigger" and "boy." He would do his best to see that none of his children would suffer this way.

Daddy King ruled the household with a firm but loving hand. He tried to teach M.L., Christine, and A.D. values and beliefs that would save them from the hardships he had endured as a poor sharecropper's son. He gave them a weekly allowance and taught them his common-sense approach to money, and he offered them spiritual guidance in the fundamentalist tradition of his church.

M.L.'s father believed deeply in God and adhered to the teachings of the Bible's Old Testament. Fundamentalists interpret Bible teachings literally. This meant that many pastimes — such as dancing or playing cards — that other people thought of as fun were considered immoral. More than once Daddy King whipped young M.L. for misbehaving. He wanted the best for his young son and wanted to be sure he would not stray from the "right" path.

Young M.L. loved, feared, and revered his father all at the same time. He and his sister and brother affectionately called their father "Daddy." For their mother, the children coined the name "Mother Dear." Their grandmother Williams, who also lived with them, was called "Mama."

Before M.L. started school, his parents did their best to protect him from racial prejudice and discrimination. They knew only too well the psychological and emotional hurt that came from prejudice. For this

14

reason, Daddy King would not allow his young children to ride in Atlanta's buses, where they would experience the humiliation of segregation. In the protected atmosphere of his home, M.L. ambitiously engaged in all healthy childhood activities. He played baseball, rode his bicycle, and more than once bounced back from near-disastrous accidents. Once his brother A.D. hit him in the head with a baseball bat! M.L. survived without a scratch.

Yet the outside world, with its split between blacks and whites, affected M.L. at an early age. He liked to play with a white boy who lived nearby. On the day in 1935 when he and his friend were to start the first grade, the two boys went to different schools. Later, the boy's parents told M.L. that because their son was white, and M.L. was black, they could no longer play together. When M.L. asked his parents about this, they told him about the history of racial discrimination. It was a heartbreaking story to tell their young son, but his parents knew that they could no longer protect M.L. from the hatred and discrimination he would encounter every day just because of the color of his skin. Still, M.L.'s parents planted the seeds of his belief that it didn't *have* to be that way, that the unequal balance between the races had to change. "You must never feel that you are less than anybody else," his mother told him. "You must always feel that you are *somebody.*"

M.L. proved to be an intelligent and ambitious youngster. He noticed that his sister, only sixteen months older than he, enjoyed certain privileges he did not. He was anxious to grow up and wanted to be able to do all the things she was able to do. When

Christine was baptized in 1934, five-year-old M.L. insisted on being baptized, too. When Christine entered school, M.L. argued that he also could go to school. But when he proudly told the teacher how old he was by holding up five fingers, he was sent home. When he finally did go to school a year later, he skipped ahead a grade, just as Christine had done.

For all his ambition, M.L. was also extremely sensitive. He developed a special fondness for his grandmother, Mama Williams, who told him he was her favorite grandchild. M.L. loved his mother and father, but it was Mama who comforted him when his father spanked him. On one occasion, M.L.'s brother, A.D., accidentally knocked Mama down while they were playing, and she lay unconscious for a few minutes. M.L. was so terrified by the sight of his silent Mama and by the shouts and frenzied actions of the family members attending to her that he ran to an upstairs window and jumped out! He was not hurt, but M.L. remained immobile on the ground until he heard that Mama had regained consciousness.

Nineteen thirty-four was a big year for M.L. In addition to being baptized, "Little Mike" King had his name changed because of Daddy King's success at Ebenezer Baptist Church. The congregation sent Daddy King to the Holy Land to visit the holy cities of Jerusalem and Bethlehem, where Jesus had spent much time preaching. Inspired by the trip, Daddy King changed his name upon his return from Michael to Martin Luther.

Martin Luther was a sixteenth-century religious reformer who challenged the church doctrine of his day and formed a new, "Protestant" church. In his zeal to do the good work of the church, Daddy King thought it appropriate to take the name of this important religious figure. Five-year-old M.L., Daddy King's namesake, had his name changed, too. When he grew older, King said it presented something of a burden to him; the work of the first Martin Luther was a big reputation to live up to.

Just as having a new name affected the way M.L. viewed himself, many black people feel that the name of their race is an important factor in how blacks are viewed, both by themselves and by others. The debate about this has gone on for hundreds of years. For example, many blacks believe they should be called "African Americans," to reflect their African heritage. For a long time "Black" and "Negro" were considered insulting and unacceptable by blacks because Spanish and Portuguese slave traders used the term. The NAACP adopted "colored people" when the organization was formed in 1908, but this also has fallen into disuse.

From an early age M.L. showed a desire to use "big words," perhaps in part because of the pressure of taking on the "big" name of Martin Luther. He told his parents, "When I grow up I'm going to get me some big words." By the time he was six years old he could recite entire passages from the Bible, and he loved to sing hymns for friends and family. He also learned to play the piano, although he did not really have the patience to master it. Before he even learned to read, M.L. displayed a gift for public speaking and a true love of language. Even though he was smart, he would always have trouble with grammar and spelling.

M.L. gave every indication that he would follow in the footsteps of his father, and this excited Daddy King. He wanted M.L. to grow up to be a preacher. Like many children, however, M.L. wanted to explore his own interests, even if they differed from his father's wishes. He described himself as "precocious" and "questioning." His brother, A.D., often openly disobeyed his father, while his sister, Christine, represented the model daughter. M.L. was somewhere in between, but he did express his own mind. As M.L. grew older, his father's ideas about how M.L. should lead his life would clash more and more directly with his own.

As a boy growing up in Atlanta, M.L. felt daily the injustices of oppression and prejudice. "Whites Only" signs faced him everywhere he went. Once when he went shopping in a department store, a white woman called him "a little nigger" and slapped him. He heard his father, a respected minister, called "boy" by whites. When M.L. was ten, the movie *Gone With the Wind* was released. The movie — a grand production set during the Civil War, and one of the first movies about the South — was greeted with much fanfare and celebration in Atlanta. Some critical observers, however, felt it reflected the prejudiced attitudes of the days when slavery was still legal — that a "good nigger" did what he or she was told and a "bad nigger" was "uppity" and talked back to whites.

M.L. was disturbed by these and other aspects of prejudice he was forced to confront. His mother and father encouraged him to be proud of himself and to love all people — whites included — even in the face of hatred. But M.L. could not understand how he could apply these values in a world that was so unfair. It seemed to him that while his father *spoke* openly about the wrongs of segregation, he did not do enough to challenge it openly on a day-to-day basis. Rather than face the hatred of whites, Daddy King avoided them, by not riding the buses, for example. As M.L. grew older, he continued to question this and other aspects of his religion and of people's behavior in general.

A family tragedy added to M.L.'s doubts in 1941, when he was twelve years old. One day, M.L. sneaked out of the house to watch a parade in downtown Atlanta. He usually studied at this time of day, but it was the middle of May and spring was in the air. His afternoon of playing hooky was interrupted when a neighbor found M.L. and told him to go straight home. M.L. returned to a house full of grief. Mama Williams had had a heart attack that afternoon and died. No one M.L. knew had ever died before, especially not someone as important to him as Mama. Hysterical with grief, he ran upstairs and, as he had done once before, jumped out a window. Although he was not hurt, when his family found him they could not console him. Mama was gone forever. M.L. cried for days after her death and could not imagine how he could go on living without her.

Mama's death filled M.L. with even more questions about the goodness of the world and his church. He wanted to believe in immortality, as the church explained it. (Baptists believe that even after death, a person's soul lives on forever.) Yet the thought that Mama's soul was in a place called heaven, as his parents assured him, did nothing to lessen the pain

19

M.L. felt. He reasoned that the religious ideas of his parents just didn't make sense if he had to endure such pain.

M.L. talked about his religious doubts in his Sunday-school class, and sometimes he even "went to the grass," or had a fistfight, when he disagreed with someone. He also competed fiercely in basketball and football games, sometimes playing so hard that his friends wondered if he was fighting rather than playing. This was, perhaps, M.L.'s way of working out his anger.

Soon after Mama's death, M.L.'s family moved to a new neighborhood in Atlanta. The family's new house on the west side of the city was in Hunter Hills, a wealthier area than the one in which they had lived before. There he began to recognize class distinctions among blacks, adding to his already painful awareness of class differences between blacks and whites. M.L. was conscious of the change in status that his new home brought, and he was eager to make his place in Hunter Hills. It was at this time that he began to take special care with his appearance and dress. One friend nicknamed him "Tweedie" because he always wore dressy tweed sport jackets.

Martin had always been a good student, and following the move to Hunter Hills he worked harder than ever to do well in school. By the time he was thirteen, in 1942, he had skipped enough grades to enter Booker T. Washington High School as a tenth-grader. He excelled at his favorite subjects, English and history, but did not feel challenged by his classes (although he continued to complain that he could not spell).

Martin Luther King, Jr.'s childhood was marked by racial discrimination and segregation. Black people, especially in the South, were considered second-class citizens. Their rights and privileges were limited, and they were forced to use facilities, such as the drinking fountains pictured here, marked "for colored only."

At the age of fifteen, when he finished high school, Martin had already discovered that his love for language and ideas made him a good public speaker. Just before graduating from high school he competed in an all-state speaking contest in a town outside Atlanta. It was a great honor, for Martin had been chosen to represent his school over many students who were older than he. A teacher, Mrs. Bradley, traveled with him to the contest to watch him present his speech on "The Negro and the Constitution." He had worked very hard on his speech, and to his great happiness and surprise he won the competition!

On the bus ride home, he talked enthusiastically with Mrs. Bradley. At one bus stop, some whites boarded and discovered that no more seats remained, so the driver asked Martin and his teacher to stand. When Martin refused, the driver called him "a black son-of-a-bitch." Only at his teacher's insistence was he finally persuaded to stand for the long ride home.

His triumph of that day had turned sour. Although he had spoken about Negroes' rights, the bus ride home only underscored how few they really had. King later said that "it was the angriest I have ever been in my life."

3

Away from Home

IN THE FALL of 1944, Martin Luther King, Jr., entered Morehouse College, a black college in Atlanta. His time at the school proved to be a liberating experience for him. Relatively free from pressure from his father, he began to explore his own ideas about the world and religion, heading down a path that would both excite and frighten him.

The summer before he began his freshman year, fifteen-year-old Martin participated in a special program sponsored by Morehouse, in which students would work on tobacco farms in Connecticut. When Martin left Georgia for Connecticut, he was on his own for the first time in his life, and he loved it!

His excitement was heightened by the differences he noticed in the way blacks were treated in the North. Like blacks in the South, most blacks in the North still suffered from poverty. Yet Martin and his friends enjoyed using the same entrance as whites at movie theaters, and sitting anywhere they pleased. In the North he could also eat at better restaurants, since they were not off limits to blacks, as they were in the South. It wasn't until the train trip back to Atlanta at the end of the summer that Martin was rudely reminded of the limits of his freedom. When he entered the dining car, a worker ushered him to the colored-only section and pulled a curtain around his table so whites would not see him.

Despite this humiliation, Martin would not forget his taste of what it was like to live in a society in which blacks and whites enjoyed the same privileges. At Morehouse, too, Martin felt as if the students did not suffer from the fear of whites with which he had grown up. Morehouse students and teachers discussed and studied how the racial inequalities that had plagued blacks for centuries could change. The president of the college, Dr. Benjamin Mays, represented the kind of man Martin admired — someone who would act on his beliefs at many levels. As a preacher he encouraged young men to be responsible and to follow their consciences. Morehouse students learned from Mays that education would free them intellectually and allow them to work toward racial equality. As an activist for social change he supported and worked for the NAACP.

Martin still resisted his father's wish that he become a preacher. At first he wanted to study medicine at Morehouse. Then he became interested in law and pursued a major in sociology, the study of society. Martin was convinced that he could do something to change the social problems that had plagued him and all black people, but he did not yet know how he could or would bring about that change.

Many of his professors helped him explore possible

avenues. Martin had a sociology professor who helped him develop his vocabulary and perfect his ability to express himself. He would answer simple questions with long and wordy sentences to show off his gift for language. For instance, his answer to a question such as "How are you?" would typically be: "I surmise that my physical equilibrium is organically quiescent." Martin was also revealing his sense of humor.

A religion professor at Morehouse discussed with Martin his uncertainty about his religion. He encouraged Martin to look beyond his doubts and see preachers as people who could be concerned about all aspects of their parishioners' lives. Too many preachers focused on their spiritual development, said this professor, instead of actively seeking to improve blacks' social and political well-being. But just because these preachers *did not* act, this did not mean that they *could not*. For the first time in his life, Martin understood what it meant to think freely about religion. Rather than merely question his religious background, he began to think of ways in which he could work *within* the church and use religion to bring about social change.

As Martin grew intellectually, he also developed in other ways. He enjoyed playing cards with friends, despite the fact that it was considered gambling and was against his religion. He also began to notice girls. His gift for language served him well when dating, and he always flattered his dates with love letters and poetry.

Meanwhile, during the summers, Martin experienced the working world. He preferred manual work to a job in an office because he wanted to learn what it was like to be a laborer. At times, the prejudice he encountered on his jobs contrasted painfully with the freedom he felt at Morehouse. He learned much about the way black workers were treated, from being called "nigger" to earning much lower wages than white laborers doing the same work.

Martin and his schoolmates talked of social change, and their sentiments seemed to be echoed all over the world. With the end of World War II in 1945, the victorious Allied countries began to reorganize and rebuild the war-torn countries in Europe. The Soviet Union, a Communist country, exerted control over Poland, Czechoslovakia, and other countries in Eastern Europe. Also at this time, colonies under the control of other countries began demanding their freedom. All over Asia and Africa, countries such as India and Algeria declared, and eventually won, their independence. In 1948, the state of Israel was created to provide a homeland for Jews, millions of whom had been murdered, along with other minorities, during World War II.

In the United States, too, it was a time of change. Black soldiers returning home wanted the army to integrate. Even though they had lived in segregated housing while overseas, they saw that European society at large was desegregated. Responding to the black soldiers' cry for equality, in 1948 President Harry S. Truman ordered the army to desegregate its barracks. This outraged some whites, and tensions between blacks and whites, especially in the South, heated up. Mobs of angry whites lynched black veterans. In one particularly violent incident, a gang of men stopped a car carrying two black couples near

Monroe, Georgia. The mob shot and killed all of them. One of the bodies had 180 bullet holes in it.

At Morehouse, Martin experimented with ways to bridge the gap between the races by serving on the Atlanta Intercollegiate Council. Working on the racially mixed council taught him that he could work with whites. The anger he had felt toward white people all his life began to be replaced by a new spirit of cooperation. He learned that throughout history blacks had attempted many solutions to the problem of racial inequality.

During the last part of the nineteenth century, when Jim Crow laws were being passed, black educator Booker T. Washington thought blacks needed to improve themselves by imitating whites. Washington believed blacks should accept segregation and concentrate on educating themselves, and that by doing this blacks might win the respect and friendship of whites.

Another black leader, Marcus Garvey, had a different idea about the future of American blacks. In the early 1900s he led a "Back to Africa" movement. Garvey believed that freedom for blacks could be won only by leaving America — a land they had been forced to come to as slaves — and settling in Africa.

W.E.B. Du Bois, who was among those who founded the NAACP, presented yet another alternative. He believed that blacks should challenge the oppressive Jim Crow laws directly, through the court system.

More recently, in the 1940s, groups such as the Congress of Racial Equality (CORE), with the help of A. Philip Randolph, founder of the powerful labor union, the Brotherhood of Sleeping Car Porters, conducted sit-ins to protest discriminatory hiring practices. Protestors staged sit-ins in stores that would not hire blacks in order to draw attention to the unfairness of the stores' hiring policies.

As Martin studied the long history of the struggle against racism, he began to develop his own ideas about how blacks could obtain equality with whites. Eventually, he came to believe that violent uprisings would only lead to more violence. One of Martin's classmates started a chapter of the NAACP at Morehouse. Although Martin would not join the NAACP until later in his life, the creation of the Morehouse chapter of the organization, among other things, caused him to wonder if his chosen career in law would put him in the best position to help blacks. Perhaps, he thought, there were other, more effective paths.

Daddy King continued to pressure Martin to pursue the ministry. He kept reminding his son that Ebenezer Baptist Church would welcome him as assistant pastor any time he felt ready. By the time Martin finished his junior year at Morehouse, his resistance to the clergy began to break down. Despite his earlier rebellion against his religious upbringing, Martin's years at Morehouse had brought him to believe that the church *could* be an effective way to work for political change. Perhaps, he finally decided, he could contribute more to society as a preacher than as a lawyer or member of some other profession.

Even so, he continued to resist his father's influence. To get away from the pressure at home, Martin returned to Connecticut during his summer break in 1947 to work in the tobacco fields, as he had done in 1944. There he could be himself and explore his independence once more. Martin was in a playful mood that summer, releasing the tensions of trying to decide what career to pursue and please his demanding father at the same time.

One night he and his friends were at a party that became so loud and disorderly that the local police were called. Worrying that his father might learn of the episode, and feeling bad that he had misbehaved, Martin was at last prompted to tell his father of his decision to go into the ministry.

Soon after Martin returned to Atlanta, Daddy King arranged for his son to deliver his first sermon at Ebenezer. The congregation responded well to the eighteen-year-old's preaching, though they thought he used too many big words. Martin did not yet have his father's presence in the pulpit, but his deep baritone voice carried through the church with conviction and authority. It was agreed that young King showed great promise. During King's last year at Morehouse, he spent a lot of time giving sermons at other churches. As he perfected his speaking style and gained confidence, King began to preach without looking at his notes.

As Martin was building up his experience, the American government was taking steps that would affect his career. Under President Truman, in 1948 the government released a report on what was known then as the "Negro question." The report used the phrase "civil rights" for the first time, and introduced the first legislative civil-rights program since Reconstruction, the national rebuilding period just after the Civil War. Truman desegregated the armed forces, and asked Congress to pass a federal law against lynchings. The cause of civil rights was not yet a popular one with the American public, but Truman's actions signaled the beginning of a new political movement for blacks.

It was in this climate of political change that King began to speak out in public on issues concerning blacks. In an article in the college newspaper he criticized Morehouse students for not using their educations properly. He felt they should actively apply their knowledge to help their fellow blacks in America. King warned that education improved minds, but that without moral convictions, even the finest minds could turn criminal. In the spring of 1948, the nineteen-year-old Martin was given the honor of delivering the Senior Sermon, a special talk given just before graduation. Then he applied to Crozer Theological Seminary in Chester, Pennsylvania.

Crozer Theological Seminary admitted people of all races. King wanted to go to school with whites to prove that his intellect and talents matched those of any student, white or black. The year King entered the seminary, Crozer attracted three students from China, a few from India and other countries around the world, and ten blacks to its class of thirty-two. This was an unusual mix of races and backgrounds in a seminary, even by today's standards.

In addition to enrolling a racially mixed class, the seminary encouraged a real sense of community and trust among its students. For example, no one was allowed to put a lock on his door. The idealistic King enthusiastically jumped into the environment at Crozer. It seemed to him the kind of atmosphere that he hoped could one day succeed in society at large.

Crozer encouraged students to question previously accepted ideas about the proper behavior for preachers. In the basement beneath the chapel, a recreation room with three pool tables and a shuffleboard court challenged his ideas about "proper" forms of recreation for a minister. He had always thought pool was a game for people of a lower class than his own, but King soon learned to love the game. Later on, when he needed to spread word to his followers during times of protest, his talent at the table would come in handy as he traveled to pool halls, where some of his followers spent their free time.

King was prompted to explore his religious beliefs even more through his study of philosophers and theologians. While at Crozer, he read the works of Walter Rauschenbusch, a Baptist minister who wrote about religion's role in freeing people from oppression. Rauschenbusch believed Christianity could serve people best when its message of brotherhood and love played an active part in their day-to-day lives. He felt the church should work for social and political change rather than preach from the pulpit in lofty terms that did not serve the people.

King also studied with a professor at Crozer who was a pacifist. Pacifists believe that physical and violent protest or taking part in war is wrong. King did not completely agree with this approach. If pacificism prevailed, he argued, might not Hitler have succeeded during World War II? However, this professor introduced King to the work of a man whose ideas on nonviolent resistance would become very important to King in the future: Mohandas Gandhi.

Gandhi led the movement to free India from British

rule by encouraging masses of people to stage peaceful protests during the 1930s and 1940s. If attacked, as they sometimes were, they did not fight back. One of Gandhi's ideas that most appealed to King was the concept of nonviolent noncooperation, or civil disobedience, which combined the force of nonviolent protest with the strength of love. According to this concept, people have a moral obligation to refuse to participate in something that they believe is wrong. Rather than strike out violently against their enemies, believers in nonviolent civil disobedience willingly go to jail for refusing to follow unjust laws. In this way, by meeting their opponents with love and nonviolence, there would be no hostility between the oppressor and the oppressed when the conflict ended. If everyone responded this way, the jails overflowing with protesters would prove how ineffective the laws were, and eventually the laws would be changed. Gandhi felt that responding to someone with hatred only created more hatred, injustice, and difference. He offered a modern example of how hatred could be met with love and love would triumph.

Gandhi was a great figure to King, especially because Gandhi's work had achieved real results — freedom for India. Gandhi had been assassinated in 1948, but even in death he continued to serve as a model to King of how blacks in America could attain equality. Also, Gandhi, like King, struggled with his own streak of violence and hatred. Gandhi's philosophy of combating hatred with love not only allowed King to work for the good of society, it helped free him from his own anger, too.

Long before he would lead other people on peaceful

protest marches, King tried to apply his nonviolent beliefs in his own life. At Crozer, as at most schools, there was a certain amount of practical joking that went on. One trick was to "raid" a student's room, making a complete mess of it. One time, a student at Crozer blamed King when his room was raided. When the student threatened to kill him, King calmly denied that he had had anything to do with the raid. Despite the fact that he had been threatened, he did not fight or press charges against the student. News of King's reaction to the angry student spread quickly across the Crozer campus, and his classmates were impressed with his action.

King became a popular student. He was active in campus activities, and during his last year he served as the student-body president. He took nine preaching courses in all at the seminary, and with this formal training he became able to use "big words" to deliver important messages to his listeners. When King preached, he filled the college chapel. He was learning to perfect both what he said and how he said it.

King began his final year at Crozer during the fall of 1950, when he was twenty-one. By the time he graduated, the following spring, he had questioned nearly every aspect of his religion and upbringing. He still was not sure what course his life would take.

Daddy King wanted his son to return to Atlanta and become the assistant pastor at Ebenezer Baptist Church, but King was not yet ready to take this step. He felt he had not learned enough and wanted to go on to graduate school to earn his doctorate in the philosophy of religion. He liked the atmosphere of school, where he could read and think about new ideas. Perhaps one day he would become a teacher himself. King talked to his mother first about how to tell his father of his decision to go to graduate school. Together, Alberta and her strong-minded son did a good job of convincing Daddy King. He gave his son his blessing to attend Boston University, and even gave him a new green Chevrolet for the ride to Boston!

About the time King went to Boston, America was becoming more concerned with the influence of communism. Following World War II, the Soviet Union and the United States, two powerful nations that had fought side by side during World War II, began what became known as the "Cold War," in which each expressed its differences about politics and society. The Soviet Union wanted to spread its kind of Communist government — with a centralized government of appointed (rather than elected) officials, and government control of industry and property — to other countries. The United States, on the other hand, believed in free enterprise, private ownership, and a government elected by the people. Poland, Czechoslovakia, and other countries were already being ruled by the Communist Soviets. The United States worried that the tide of Soviet communism would spread to other countries, and in 1947, President Harry Truman set about stopping the expansion of communism in the world. One result of that strategy was that American soldiers were sent to Korea with United Nations forces in order to help South Korea defend itself against invading forces from communist North Korea.

By 1950, some people in the United States worried that communism's influence reached too far inside America's own borders. With the relatively new medium of television (President Truman delivered the first coast-to-coast broadcast in the fall of 1951), America watched Senator Joseph McCarthy lead an attack on many Americans who were accused of being connected with the Communist Party in the United States.

King was sympathetic to the idea of all people sharing equally in a society. Some of the people who would become his future associates in the civil-rights movement were even members of the Communist Party. But King did not agree with all of the party's ideas. He felt that communism's view of the world was too material, that it did not address people's spiritual needs.

Even as he kept pace with world events, King immersed himself in his studies at Boston University. He wanted to be accepted as an intellectual by his professors and fellow students. He changed the way he signed his name to make it look more distinguished, and began to smoke a pipe. In addition to his courses at Boston University, he took classes at Harvard University on philosophers such as Soren Kierkegaard, Martin Heidegger, and Jean-Paul Sartre.

King and a few of the small number of black students there formed the Dialectical Society, or Philosophical Club, to discuss their work at school. To maintain his image as an intellectual, King did not write about racial topics, nor did he actively fight racism as he had at Morehouse and Crozer. He and some of the other black students felt that their work would not be taken as seriously by white teachers or students if they wrote about civil rights.

The members of the Dialectical Society did occasionally bring up civil rights issues, however, and were even able to discuss them with some humor.

Late one night King said with a serious look on his face that he had led a funeral the previous weekend. "We buried Jim," he said.

"Jim who?" asked one of the students.

"Jim Crow," King answered, referring to the name for the segregation laws. "Yeah, we did Jim up real good. We put him to rest."

King also found time for fun and amusement, and like most young men his age, he dated often. One day early in 1952, when King mentioned that he would like to meet a girl from the South, a friend suggested he call a young woman named Coretta Scott, who was from Alabama. King called Coretta and somehow convinced her to have lunch with him the next day.

Martin was now twenty-three years old. He was ready to marry, and he liked Coretta. Her character, intelligence, personality, and beauty were all the qualities he wanted in a wife. The daughter of a farmer from rural Alabama, she had picked cotton on her father's farm as a child, and had later attended Antioch College in Ohio. When King met her, she was a student at the New England Conservatory of Music, and she wanted to be a classical singer.

Daddy King, who thought his son ought to be married by now, had been pressuring him to find a wife for some time. When Coretta visited the Kings in Atlanta that August, however, the senior King did not take her seriously as a wife for his son. At twenty-five, she was two years older than Martin and from a farmer's family. Daddy King wanted his son to marry a woman from their own affluent West Side neighborhood in Atlanta.

During the fall of 1952, Martin's parents visited

him in Boston, and Daddy King spoke sternly to both his son and Coretta about why they should not marry. Pulling his mother aside, Martin told her he would marry Coretta, no matter what his father said. The next day, when Daddy King started in once more about Martin's not getting married, Martin replied calmly that he would marry Coretta after getting his degree. Daddy took a moment to let his son's words sink in. Martin's determination must have finally gotten through, for Daddy King then slammed his fist down on a table and said, "Now, you two had better get married!" Daddy King himself performed the ceremony, on June 18, 1953.

Coretta proved to be the perfect wife for a young preacher. She was talented, smart, outgoing, and good at remembering people's names after meeting them only once. King's friends agreed that she put people at ease and was always polite. King loved her ability to discuss ideas with him, yet he also believed that his career should come first in both their lives. At the time, it was generally accepted that in a marriage the husband was the head of the household, while the wife took care of the home and family. Although Coretta wanted to go on singing, she also realized how important it was to her husband that she take on the traditional role of being his wife. The decision was difficult for Coretta, but eventually she agreed that after finishing her studies, she would give up her singing career and devote herself to their home and children. Thus, within the guidelines of a traditional marriage, they began a happy partnership.

4

Montgomery

AFTER MARTIN AND Coretta married, they settled into a routine in Boston. In order to receive his doctoral degree from Boston University, Martin still had to write his dissertation, a big final essay that would complete his graduate work. Coretta had to complete thirteen courses before she would receive her degree at the New England Conservatory of Music. Though Martin was head of the household, he shared the responsibilities of their home life with Coretta that first year. He cleaned the apartment and did the laundry, and one night a week he cooked their dinner. One of his favorite meals was smothered cabbage, pork chops, and pigs' feet.

The couple planned to stay in Boston until Coretta finished her music degree in the spring of 1954. Early that year, King looked for teaching jobs, and also went south to look for a pastorship, preaching a few trial sermons at churches there.

One of the churches he visited was the Dexter Avenue Baptist Church in Montgomery, Alabama. It was small, but it had a good reputation. Upon arriving in Montgomery for his visit to Dexter, King stopped at the home of Ralph Abernathy, the pastor of the city's First Baptist Church. Abernathy, who was a friend of the previous pastor of Dexter, invited King to join his family for dinner. Around a table piled high with steak and onions, turnip greens, cornbread, and other delicious fare, they talked and laughed. Abernathy gave King advice on becoming a preacher at Dexter. That night, the two men struck up a close friendship that would last for the rest of King's life.

The Dexter congregation received King's trial sermon enthusiastically. Within weeks, Dexter offered King a position he could not refuse. Just twenty-five years old, he would earn a yearly salary of $4,200, more money than any other black pastor in Montgomery. Although he had not yet completed his graduate work, King accepted the offer on April 14, 1954, and he and Coretta moved to Montgomery in September.

Coretta wanted to stay in the North. Montgomery was much smaller than Boston and had only a small black business district consisting of a gas station and a few stores. In Boston, she sang hymns at a white Presbyterian church and new music at the New England Conservatory. It was unlikely she would enjoy such opportunities in the deeply segregated city of Montgomery. However, Coretta had agreed that her husband would be head of the household, and in the end the decision to go to Montgomery received her full support.

King and Abernathy faced some difficult times in Montgomery. The nation was going through many changes. In May 1954, the U.S. Supreme Court ruled in *Brown v. Board of Education* that school segregation was unconstitutional. The landmark case was very important to the civil-rights movement, and it strengthened the NAACP's efforts to enroll students at previously segregated schools. But the ruling was unpopular in the South, and only added to the general climate of dissatisfaction that prevailed there after the Korean conflict ended without a U.S. victory. The United States had failed in its attempt to subdue Communist forces in North Korea, and the nation's image suffered a blow when the war ended in a stalemate in 1953.

Furthermore, with the election in 1952 of Dwight D. Eisenhower as President of the United States, civil-rights leaders had a new government to deal with. Eisenhower met with black leaders and hired the first black professional, E. Frederic Morrow, for the White House staff. But before becoming president, he had served for forty years in a segregated army and felt uncomfortable with blacks. He desegregated Washington's public facilities and supported the *Brown* decision, but his support was quiet. Unlike his predecessor, Harry Truman, Eisenhower felt civil rights was too unpopular an issue for him to back with the full power of his position.

Nonetheless, King approached his new pastorship at Dexter with enthusiasm. He combined the practical, common-sense training of his father with the philosophical beliefs he had developed during his years in school. When King first addressed his new congregation, he presented them with a plan for increasing the church's income. He also called upon every member of his church to register to vote. In 1954, this was no easy task in Alabama. Local government officials made registration nearly impossible for blacks, and fewer than 5 percent of Alabama's blacks could vote. King also formed a committee that would educate Dexter members about politics and encourage them to join the NAACP.

During his first year at Dexter, King established the hectic work schedule from which he would find relief only a few times in his life. He awoke at five-thirty every morning and worked on his doctoral dissertation until nine. Then he began his busy day of visiting with church members and other pastors in Montgomery. In addition to fulfilling the round-the-clock role of a pastor, King found time to attend NAACP meetings and become active in the political life of Montgomery.

His popularity as a preacher spread. In 1954 he traveled to Boston twice to work on his Ph.D., stopping on the way there and back to preach at several churches and colleges. Gradually his preaching style changed. Trained in the formal method of speaking in public, he soon learned to sense the reaction of his audience. He would deliver a line and wait for their response before moving on to his next point. He would fall into a rhythm with the congregation, pulling them along with the force and tempo of his words. He did not shout, but he delivered his words so passionately that listeners often felt that he *was* shouting. When he greeted the members of his congregation after the service, he treated each member as if he or she were the only person who mattered, inquiring how each one was doing and asking about specific family concerns.

At home, the newlyweds wasted no time starting

their family. King earned his doctorate in July 1955, and their first daughter, Yolanda, was born in November. King loved their new baby and doted proudly on her, but he felt Yolanda Denise was too long and difficult a name for many to pronounce. Coretta wanted to keep the name, so the couple compromised by coming up with the shorter nickname of Yoki.

Soon after Yoki's birth, King decided to become more involved in the NAACP. Following the Supreme Court's *Brown* ruling, the NAACP filed more and more suits demanding desegregation, and tensions between whites and blacks heightened throughout the south. King had already been appointed to the executive committee of the NAACP's local chapter, and now he wanted to run for president. Coretta and her mother-in-law tried to discourage him, arguing that he already maintained a busy schedule and had a child to think about, too. Before King had a chance to decide what to do, however, events in Montgomery led him toward a central role in fighting whites' opposition to desegregation.

A few blacks in Montgomery had been arrested for refusing to move to the back of the bus during King's first two years in Montgomery. E.D. Nixon, a prominent labor leader who was head of the local branch of the NAACP, watched these arrests with interest. He and a group called the Black Women's Political Council wanted to challenge Montgomery's bus segregation laws in the courts, and they were on the lookout for the right "test case." Thursday, December 1, 1955 provided them with just what they were looking for.

Rosa Parks, a seamstress and secretary of the local

NAACP chapter, was taking the bus home after a long day's work. The bus was crowded, and when the bus driver ordered Mrs. Parks to give her seat to a white man, she refused. The driver, who was in charge of enforcing the segregation codes on the bus, arrested her.

When Rosa Parks's mother called E.D. Nixon about her arrest, Nixon knew he had his test case. A quiet, hard-working woman, Mrs. Parks could gain the sympathy of the many black groups in Montgomery. She was educated enough to appeal to middle-class blacks, yet she herself was working-class. In Montgomery, where few black leaders or groups could agree on how — or even if — the civil-rights struggle should be fought, Rosa Parks would offer an ideal image to blacks from all backgrounds. Once Nixon bailed Mrs. Parks out of jail and received her permission to go ahead with her case, he quickly called Montgomery's black leaders, including Dr. Martin Luther King, Jr., to inform them of what was happening.

The night of Rosa Parks's arrest, the Women's Political Council met to do its part in organizing a massive protest to support her case. In a letter which the council distributed throughout the city, it asked blacks to boycott the buses on Monday morning, the day of Mrs. Parks's trial. Fifty black leaders met in the basement of the Dexter Avenue Baptist Church that weekend, and they wrote another version of the letter written by the Women's Council. By Saturday, thousands of leaflets had been spread throughout the black community. On Sunday the preachers announced the boycott from their pulpits to be sure word got out. Even Robert Graetz, the only white pastor of a black church, publicized the boycott.

The air was alive with tension and anticipation on the morning of Monday, December 5. Since most of the city's blacks did not own cars, they usually depended on the buses to get to work. Boycotting the buses meant that they would have to walk or take taxis. Would they heed the call to avoid the buses? They did. As King drove through Montgomery's streets he saw that all the buses were almost completely empty!

That day, the court convicted Rosa Parks, and her lawyer filed an appeal. A mass meeting was scheduled for Monday night to discuss what had happened and how they should proceed. Before the meeting, King met with Nixon, Abernathy, and another minister to compose a list of demands to present to the leaders of the city of Montgomery. When it was suggested that they work on the list without using their names in order to avoid harassment from whites, King spoke up and insisted that they should act openly. The small group formed an official organization, the Montgomery Improvement Association (MIA), to lead the boycott, and chose King to head the organization. The creators of the MIA remembered King's willingness to speak out. Here was a man who would not hesitate to speak his mind, and who had not been in Montgomery long enough to make any real enemies. These qualities made him a good choice for heading the organization.

King, at the age of twenty-six, found himself at the center of one of Montgomery's — and America's —

first major civil-rights protests. Hurrying home before the mass meeting, King told Coretta about the creation of the MIA and quickly wrote his first protest speech. He worried that his wife might be critical of his decision to play such a major role in the negotiations. A boycott would make the white community angry and could result in violence. But Coretta quietly told him that she supported this new work. She knew how important the boycott could be to securing equal rights for blacks in Montgomery.

Though the one-day boycott succeeded, the new MIA did not know if it could rally the support to continue the protest. The crowd's response at that night's mass meeting would tell them. When King returned to the Holt Street Baptist Church, where the meeting had already begun, he had to push his way through the hundreds of people who surrounded the church. Blacks all over the city knew that that day's boycott had been successfully carried out. Such a protest had never been attempted before in Montgomery, and everyone wanted to see what would happen next. Every seat in the church was filled.

King stepped up to the pulpit to speak. When he began, the crowd was quiet. As King continued, his deep voice rising and falling with the rhythm of his words, a few cries of "Yes!" and "Amen!" answered him from the crowd. Soon he had the whole room following his words as he spoke of the reason for their gathering. They would challenge the unjust segregation laws. Speaking of Rosa Parks, he said, "Nobody can doubt the height of her character, nobody can doubt the depth of her Christian commitment. And

just because she refused to get up, she was arrested."
The audience was really with him then. Everyone in
the church cheered when he said, "And you know,
my friends, there comes a time when people get tired
. . . of being kicked about by the brutal feet of oppression."

The cheers swelled to thunderous applause. Even
the people standing outside began cheering and
applauding. Inside, the floor rumbled as people
began stamping their feet. When the church finally
quieted, King continued with his message of nonviolence. If they resorted to violence, he said, they
would be no better than the Ku Klux Klan and other
hateful whites. Violence was unjust, he told them,
and they did not intend to answer one injustice —
segregation — with another. They would persuade
whites with *nonviolent* protest until justice won the
battle.

King's first protest speech was a success. He encouraged his listeners to continue the boycott until
the buses were desegregated, but he warned them
that there were long, difficult days ahead. On the first
day of the boycott, sympathetic taxi drivers had
taken many people to work, charging a reduced fare.
A week later, the police commissioner threatened to
arrest cab drivers who charged less than the full fare
to protestors. The MIA quickly organized a massive
car pool. The organization needed to provide 20,000
rides a day. When King called on supporters of the
boycott to volunteer for the car pool, 150 people
signed up to help.

Boycotting the buses meant that the city's bus
company would lose a huge amount of money. As the

boycott continued, the city's buses lost between 30,000 and 40,000 fares a day. But even with the threat of so much lost revenue, Montgomery's White Citizens' Council did not want the mayor or the bus company to give in to the MIA's demands. As in cities all over the South, the council had been formed by leading white citizens to ensure that the "Southern" way of life — in other words, segregation — would prevail. Negotiations between the two groups began seven days after the Rosa Parks arrest and came to an abrupt halt on December 20. Neither side would consent to the other's wishes.

Despite the strain of walking to work or waiting for a ride in the car pool, the boycott continued. Every night, people met at mass meetings to renew their strength and hear encouraging speeches from King and other MIA leaders. The boycott affected young and old alike. One older woman, Mother Pollard, walked to work despite her frail condition. In one speech, King told his listeners the story of how someone had suggested that Mother Pollard should be allowed to ride the bus. When she was told she could ride the bus, King recounted, Mother Pollard's reply offered inspiration to all of them: "My feet is tired, but my soul is rested."

By January 1956, more than a month into the boycott, the city's bus company warned city officials that they would soon run out of money. The MIA was also struggling to make ends meet, but it had accomplished much. By now 350 cars were participating in the car pool. Montgomery's newspaper, the *Advertiser*, interviewed King and published an article about him. MIA leaders knew their boycott had hit a sore spot with whites if they could get an entire story on a black leader in a white newspaper!

King's happiness about the article was dimmed when he learned that the *Advertiser* planned to publish an article saying that the city and black leaders had reached a settlement to end the boycott. King knew no agreement had been reached, but he also knew that some blacks thought the boycott had lasted too long. Rather than continue the boycott, they wanted the NAACP to step in and take the case to court. Could the MIA have been betrayed by those who supported this idea?

On Saturday, January 21, King finally found out what this "settlement" was: The city commissioners had reached an agreement with just three preachers who weren't even from Montgomery but from towns outside the city. If the article appeared in the *Advertiser* the next day, as it was supposed to, and people believed a true settlement had been reached, the boycott might fall apart. King and the others had to find a way of letting all Montgomery's blacks know that the boycott still lived, that this supposed pact was really a sham.

They decided to call all the black preachers and ask them to make announcements in their churches. Then King figured out a way to let those who might not make it to church know about the false news of an agreement. With a small group of friends, he drove through the countryside visiting black "juke joints," bars where people met to drink, dance, and play pool. King's "sinful" habit of playing pool came in handy as he rushed to save the boycott. Their efforts must have been successful, for on Monday morning, the buses remained empty, despite the publication of the article.

After six weeks of empty buses, the city grew desperate to break the spirit of the protesters. Police began stopping the car-pool drivers and ticketing them for minor traffic violations. Often the police made up false violations just to continue the harassment. One woman received seventeen tickets by the time the boycott was over. King was arrested, too, and went to jail for the first time in his life. He was so shaken by his arrest and by the news of the false agreement that had appeared in the *Advertiser* that he felt he was failing as the MIA's leader. Even in his triumphant moments, King sometimes doubted his skill as a leader. In this case, he even offered to resign, but the MIA unanimously voted to reject the offer.

With renewed strength, King went on to attack segregation on Montgomery buses from a new angle. Since the beginning of the boycott, the NAACP had maintained that it would be better to fight discrimination through the courts (although the head of the NAACP, Roy Wilkins, did send a contribution to the MIA). Late in January, King and other MIA leaders decided to go along with the idea. Through the NAACP they filed a lawsuit in federal court that challenged bus segregation in Montgomery. The MIA would continue the boycott at the same time. One way or the other, they hoped to force the city to give in to their demands.

Though the NAACP and King's organization finally cooperated in Montgomery, differences between various black groups would haunt King's career as a civil-rights leader. The NAACP would often disagree with King's protest methods; it preferred to work *within* the system to bring about change, while King pushed to change the system from the outside.

King and his family had received numerous threats of violence since the beginning of the boycott. On January 30, someone made good on the threat. As King announced the plans for the lawsuit at the mass meeting, someone brought the message that his house had just been bombed. King knew that Coretta and Yoki were at home. Could they have been hurt, or even killed? Stunned, King inquired about his wife and daughter. Learning that they had survived the blast unhurt, he quickly ended the meeting and urged the people to go home quietly and peacefully.

Shaking with concern for his family, King rushed home. A large, angry crowd of his supporters waited outside. Some were waving broken bottles and were ready to fight those responsible for the bombing. The tempers of police on the scene were rising, too, and it seemed as if there might be a confrontation. King made his way across what used to be his front porch, where the bomb had exploded, and entered the house. Glass littered the living room just inside, and Coretta, still in her bathrobe, waited for her husband in the back of the house with their daughter. King hugged them. Still in shock, the reality of the bombing seemed to sink in as he told her, "Thank God you and the baby are all right!" Though shaken by his family's encounter with violence, King still acted the part of a leader. He quietly asked Coretta to get dressed. They would have to stay somewhere else for the night.

While King was inside with Coretta and Yoki, the crowd outside had worked itself up into a frenzy. Why did King stay inside so long? Were Coretta and his baby hurt? Someone in the crowd shouted for King; the people wanted to know what was happening. King went out onto the now-damaged porch. Calmly, he asked the crowd to go home. "I want you to love our enemies," he told them. "Be good to them. This is what we must live by. We must meet hate with love."

But the crowd could not be calmed. Where was Coretta? Might King be hiding the fact that she was hurt? King called his wife outside. He needed her help to calm the crowd, and he needed her by his side for support. When Coretta joined him on the porch to show the people that she truly was not hurt, the crowd slowly dispersed and went home. Later, when the Kings had settled in at a friend's house for the night, Martin thanked Coretta for being so strong through the night's confusion. As strong as he had appeared in public, he still needed her.

With the filing of the NAACP lawsuit and news of violence in Montgomery, the bus boycott became known to people all over the country. One person who became interested in King's nonviolent approach to the boycott was Bayard Rustin. Rustin had learned to be a good organizer first as a member of the Young Communist League while attending college. He had learned about direct-action protest as a member of a pacifist organization and as an early member of the Congress of Racial Equality (CORE). He had participated in protests against segregation in the South in 1947. Rustin, who also believed in Gandhi's philosophy of accepting the punishment of one's oppressors, served time in prison following his arrest for breaking local segregation laws. After he left prison he went to India to study Gandhi's work. He had been watching the progress of King and the Montgomery boycotters, and was eager to show them how they could employ Gandhi's nonviolent techniques more effectively.

Rustin arrived in Montgomery on February 21, 1956, just as the city warned boycott leaders they would be arrested if they continued their protest. King was in Nashville, Tennessee, at the time, at a speaking engagement. His popularity had grown all over the South. As important as he was to the MIA, he still found time to accept speaking invitations. This way he could broaden support for Montgomery's protest. With Rustin's advice and encouragement, Ralph Abernathy and the other MIA leaders decided they would go ahead with the boycott in the face of the city's warning, even if they had to go to jail.

When King got word of the city's warning, he flew to Atlanta to pick up Coretta and Yoki, who visited there while he spoke in Nashville. Daddy King and other prominent Atlanta leaders tried to convince his son to stay in Atlanta until things calmed down in Montgomery. What good would it do to get arrested? When young King could not be convinced, Daddy King burst into tears. King, Jr., did receive the support of one man: Dr. Benjamin Mays, King's college mentor and president of Morehouse College. With Dr. Mays's help, the NAACP pledged to support King and to help defend him in court if he were arrested.

Back in Montgomery, other MIA leaders were already going to jail. In fact, the leaders actually sought out their punishment. Much to the surprise of city officials, first E.D. Nixon, then dozens of other black leaders, went to the jail to say they were ready to be arrested. When King arrived at the jail, on February 22, a crowd gathered to encourage and cheer him on. At the mass meeting that night it was announced that the next day would be "Double-P Day," a day of prayer and pilgrimage in support of the jailed leader. Everyone would walk to work rather than car pool.

Thirty-five reporters attended the mass meeting the night of the arrests. Even *The New York Times* covered the meeting and published an article about King. The reporters' stories brought financial support and encouragement to the young protest movement. By March 1956, when King's trial began, reporters from all over the world were covering the story. By the time he was convicted and sentenced to a $500 fine, King had emerged as a civil-rights figure of national renown.

The boycott continued through the summer of 1956. The young Dr. King now realized he could draw on the support of sympathetic whites and blacks alike all over the country. Among these was Harry Belafonte, a black singer who would soon release his first million-selling album. With its new prominence and funding, the MIA was able to buy its own cars for the car pool. The group's strength, however, offered another legal opening for its opponents in the city government. Since the MIA purchased a fleet of cars specifically for taking boycotters to work, instead of using people's private cars, the city wanted to prosecute the organization for running an unlicensed municipal transportation system. This legal challenge threatened to cripple the organization's efforts.

The MIA was saved from prosecution on November 13, when the U.S. Supreme Court ruled that bus segregation was unconstitutional. King and the other civil-rights leaders had won! Jubilant blacks celebrated all over the city, and leaders of the boycott rode in victory on a Montgomery bus. Toward the front of the bus, King sat next to Robert Graetz, a Baptist pastor and the only white minister to support the MIA boycott. The moment symbolized their own victory as well as the beginning of the end of segregation all over the South. The victorious end to the boycott offered a model of hope and success to people everywhere.

5

1,000 Speeches

INSPIRED BY THE Montgomery victory, King pursued his dream of spreading the civil-rights movement to other cities in the South. Speaking invitations poured in, and King began a hectic travel schedule. But he still had much to learn about organizing widespread protests. King was unsure of his new role as a civil-rights leader, but he forged ahead bravely, taking the podium in city after city. During the next few years, he would travel all over the world gathering support for the movement and learning as much as he could about nonviolent protest.

In January 1957, King met with about sixty preachers from states all over the South at the first Negro Leaders Conference on Nonviolent Integration in Atlanta. This meeting was important because it led to the organization of the Southern Christian Leadership Conference (SCLC). With King as its president, the SCLC would sponsor and organize many civil-rights protests in the years to come.

Meanwhile, opposition to the civil-rights movement

continued to be fierce. The end of the Montgomery boycott had sparked hatred among whites who were against integration. In late 1956, soon after U.S. marshals served Montgomery city officials with notices that they must end bus segregation, angry whites fired gunshots at integrated buses. A fifteen-year-old black girl was beaten at a bus stop. On January 10, 1957, the day the black leaders met at the Atlanta conference, bombs exploded at four churches and two houses, including Abernathy's, in Montgomery.

Though King and other black preachers organized to continue the struggle for desegregation, the outburst of violence upset King. Violence threatened him and his family and, worse, it threatened the safety of Montgomery blacks who looked to him for leadership and support. To further upset matters, the MIA leaders, no longer focused on the boycott that kept them united, could not agree on a new plan.

Characteristically, King blamed himself for the MIA's difficulties and for the harm that came to his supporters. At a mass meeting in Montgomery after the bombings, King's emotions overcame him. He prayed that no one would have to die because of the struggle for freedom, exclaiming, "If anyone has to die, let it be me!" Listeners immediately began shouting in protest; they weren't about to let the leader of their movement ask God to allow him to die. The response so overwhelmed King that he was unable to continue speaking. The crowd fell silent and still he could not go on. After a few moments, two other preachers led King away from the pulpit.

Two weeks later, King's doubts about his effectiveness as a nonviolent leader were aggravated still further. He received a particularly threatening phone call at home that gave him the feeling that something would happen again. Coretta and Yoki were in Atlanta with King's relatives at the time. His friend Bob Williams who had also attended Morehouse and who was a fellow civil-rights activist, was with him that night. The two went to Williams's house. A few hours later, a bomb went off, ruining the front of King's house.

Nonetheless, King would not give up his fight to free blacks from discrimination. Early in 1957, he appeared on the cover of *Time* magazine, an honor for anyone. He also told *The New York Times Magazine* that perhaps now he had earned the right to use the name of Martin Luther. King seemed to realize that he was embarking on a path that would change American life forever.

As King set out to build his new organization, the SCLC, his aims were two-fold: to expand his network of supporters, and to learn more about planning protests. King realized that the nonviolent boycott in Montgomery had occurred not because of any well-thought-out strategy, but because of his own feelings that he should not attack or hate his enemies. He wanted to ensure that the SCLC would act according to a careful, organized plan.

MIA leaders had learned from Bayard Rustin that Gandhi's technique of accepting punishment from one's opponents was an effective instrument of change. Not surprisingly, King now turned to Rustin for training some of the SCLC members in protesting. As he traveled around the country on speaking engagements, he met other leaders who added their wisdom and experience. Among these were Stanley

Levison, a lawyer who had lots of experience as a fund-raiser and organizer, and James Lawson, who had traveled in India and Africa to work with nonviolent resisters there. Levison would become King's closest white friend and "money man." Lawson would train hundreds of students in nonviolent techniques through the Student Nonviolent Coordinating Committee (SNCC). King's network began to fall into place.

With Levison and Bayard Rustin's help, King and the SCLC decided to pressure President Eisenhower about voting-rights laws and the proposed 1957 Civil Rights Act. The act would be the first civil-rights legislation in eighty-two years, and much debate and politicking surrounded its wording. By the time Congress passed it in August, the Act had been toned down to make it more "acceptable" to civil-rights opponents, and included amendments that would actually *hurt* the civil-rights movement. For instance, it said that state officials accused of violating voting rights could be tried in state court, rather than federal. Black leaders knew that no Southern jury would convict a state official for violating the voting rights of a black person.

The proposed Civil Rights Act was a blow to King. During a visit to Ghana the previous March, he had witnessed the liberation of a whole country — in 1957 Ghana had become the first African country to achieve independence since the founding of Liberia in 1847. As he and Coretta traveled through Rome, Geneva, Paris, and London on their way home, people everywhere speculated about which African colony would next win its independence. It seemed to King that in the democratic society of America the same could happen for blacks. But he was finding that true freedom for blacks in America would not come easily.

King tried to meet with President Eisenhower to talk about the Civil Rights Act, but Eisenhower refused. To put pressure on the administration, King, Rustin, and NAACP head Roy Wilkins planned a prayer pilgrimage to Washington, D.C. Eisenhower initially resisted approving the march, but through some clever political moves, Wilkins convinced the President to allow it.

On May 17, 1957, the third anniversary of the *Brown v. Board of Education* decision to desegregate the nation's schools, some 30,000 people gathered on the steps of the Lincoln Memorial. Preachers involved in the movement and entertainers such as Sammy Davis, Jr., Sidney Poitier, and Harry Belafonte addressed the crowd. King, as the main speaker, spoke last. "Give us the ballot!" he repeated again and again, and the crowd responded enthusiastically. The press noted that the triumphant speech placed King firmly among the leaders of the growing civil-rights movement.

But the march did not persuade Congress to pass a strong civil-rights act, and President Eisenhower still would not meet with black leaders. (Eisenhower would not meet with black leaders until June 1958.) Frustrated by his fruitless efforts in Washington, King now believed that blacks should not rely on the white-dominated Eisenhower administration in the struggle for racial equality. Black groups could count only on themselves to fight for civil rights.

In September 1957, Eisenhower finally acted to

protect civil rights when the state of Arkansas refused to admit nine black students to a Little Rock high school. The governor of Arkansas violated federal law by keeping out the black students. Eisenhower forced the state to obey the law by sending in army paratroopers and the Arkansas National Guard to protect the students. It was the first time since Reconstruction that a president sent federal troops to overrule a state segregation law, and the event marked a turning point in civil-rights history.

This was also the first civil-rights event to be covered by television news reporters. Cameras showed the National Guardsmen and captured the ugly scene as mobs of white students surrounded the black students and taunted them. Television pictures of the movement's dignified, nonviolent response sent a powerful message to millions of people all over the world. In fact, many historians have observed that without television cameras, the civil-rights struggle may not have evolved as it did.

King's SCLC continued its fight against discrimination with a voter-registration campaign. The aim was to register 2 million black voters before the next presidential election, in 1960. Traveling from city to city, King spoke in order to raise money for the campaign. One magazine estimated that King traveled 780,000 miles a year from 1957 to 1959 to meet his hectic schedule of four speaking engagements a week. In that time he is said to have given an estimated 1,000 speeches!

Still, King felt he needed to do even more to get his message out to more people. With this in mind, he began his first book, *Stride Toward Freedom*, with the help of black historian L.D. Reddick. The book told the story of the Montgomery boycott and was to be published in 1958.

King now had the responsibilities of three important roles: civil-rights leader, family man, and pastor. He became so consumed with his work that he was not able to be at the hospital when his second child, Martin Luther King III, was born in October 1957. King was running a business meeting at Dexter when a messenger brought the news to him. He gleefully shared his news, and after the cheers died down he continued with the meeting as if everything were business as usual.

King soon found himself in the spotlight once again. On August 29, 1958, someone tried to kill Ralph Abernathy. On September 3, the day of his attacker's preliminary hearing at the Montgomery courthouse, King and Coretta tried to attend. When a guard refused to let King into the courtroom, King asked to see Abernathy's lawyer. The guard and another court officer grabbed King and pushed him out of the courthouse to take him to jail. As they made their way down the street, one of the guards twisted King's arm behind his back. Though King did not struggle with the police, his body twisted as they continued to hold his arm behind his back. At that moment, a photographer saw what was happening and began taking pictures. The pictures eventually went out to every news organization over the international wire services, and as a result King received an outpouring of support he hadn't seen since the mass arrests during the Montgomery boycott. The next day King was convicted of loitering and told he could pay a $14 fine or serve fourteen days in jail. He wanted to go to jail, but Police Commissioner Clyde Sellers, who did not want King to get the publicity that a jail term would bring, paid his fine and freed him.

Taking advantage of renewed public attention, King left for New York later in September to promote his book. He appeared on the "Today" show and later went to Blumstein's department store in Harlem to sign copies of the book. It seemed to be the perfect publicity event. A small crowd of admirers surrounded King, and a photographer took pictures of him with NAACP president Roy Wilkins.

Then a noisy, aggressive woman pushed through the crowd toward King and asked him if he was really Martin Luther King. When he said yes, she quickly pulled a sharpened letter opener from her coat and, before anyone knew what had happened, stabbed King in the chest. Quickly, the crowd fell around the injured leader to protect him, while his attacker was held back. Fortunately, King did not try to remove the knife from his chest, and kept still until the ambulance arrived. He learned later that the blade had lodged against the aorta, the body's largest artery. The slightest movement could have caused him to bleed to death. Doctors said if he had so much as sneezed that he wouldn't have lived through the ordeal. The woman, forty-two-year-old Izola Ware Curry of Georgia, was caught at the scene; she was found to have an automatic pistol in her possession. She was subsequently diagnosed as a paranoid schizophrenic and taken to a hospital for the mentally ill.

Shaken by the attack, King began to doubt himself again. The voter registration drive was not going well.

The SCLC needed money and had few volunteers to recruit the millions that the organization had pledged to register. In addition, many of the movement's recent protest demonstrations and marches were not as successful as King would have liked. Still, black leaders continued to compliment the job King was doing. Coretta noted that her husband felt guilty about receiving praise for actions that to him did nothing to further the cause of American blacks. After all, he had been stabbed while promoting his own book, not leading a boycott or a march.

In February 1959, King and Coretta journeyed to India. On their arrival in Bombay, they were supposed to be greeted by Prime Minister Jawaharlal Nehru, but because they were delayed in Zurich, Nehru was no longer in Bombay when they arrived. Instead of being driven in a limousine, the Kings ended up taking a bus into the city from the airport. King was appalled at the poverty he witnessed on the ride. He and Coretta finally met with Nehru a day later in Delhi, India's capital, where Nehru treated them to a lavish dinner. For hours, King and Nehru discussed Indian and American politics, nonviolence, and race questions.

Returning to Bombay, the Kings stayed in the house Gandhi had called home whenever he was in the city. Conditions there were different from what the Kings were used to. Gandhi had lived without material possessions, and the house had no modern conveniences such as heat and hot water. But the Kings did not complain; the many homeless people they saw there, and other aspects of life in India, were continuing to make a deep impression.

For King the trip to India was inspirational. India had become independent as a result of nonviolent protest. King met many of Gandhi's followers, who continued to spread the word of Gandhi's philosophy by living and acting as he had. King came to believe again that he could use Gandhi's philosophy effectively in America's struggle to free oppressed people.

King returned home in time to speak at a "Youth March on Washington," on April 18, 1959. However, like many recent civil-rights protests, the march did not attract much attention. The movement seemed to be at a standstill.

More than two years had passed since King's success in Montgomery. Though he could claim no direct advances for civil rights in that time, he had learned a valuable lesson traveling all over the world and delivering his speeches. He found that the movement needed more than his unquestioned talent for inspiring a crowd. He met people who would prove to be key players in the years ahead. He attracted the attention of political and financial supporters and tasted the difficulties of Washington politics. He had begun to build a public image. Now he wanted to use that image to put his ideas and vision for the future into practice.

6

Freedom Now

WHEN KING RETURNED from India he realized he could not effectively lead both the SCLC and attend to his duties as Dexter's pastor. The SCLC voter-registration campaign had registered only a fraction of the voters it needed. King was now thirty years old. For years, associates had tried to convince him to devote all his efforts to the civil rights movement. Late in 1959, he finally had to admit he could not continue at Dexter.

On the last Sunday in November, he told the Dexter congregation that he would leave two months later, on the last Sunday of January 1960. He explained to them that he was too worn out from his busy schedule to give all that they should expect from a pastor. Later, he told the press that he felt now was the time for advances in civil rights. He was leaving his church to devote himself to that cause.

The Kings then decided to move back to Atlanta. Though Atlanta lay in the heart of the segregated South, King knew he would find support there among black leaders. Daddy King hoped that his son would join him at the Ebenezer Baptist Church. Martin resisted at first, but he finally agreed that they would become co-pastors of Ebenezer. King, Jr., would draw the crowds, while King, Sr., would see to the church's daily management.

Rather than return to Atlanta's wealthier West Side, where Daddy King lived, Martin and his family moved into the poorer East Side of Atlanta. King's salary from the SCLC would be only $1 a year; to that Ebenezer added a modest $6,000. The Kings would never live the way Gandhi had, but their life-style would remain simple.

As Martin bade his fond farewells to Dexter, students in Greensboro, North Carolina, staged the first of many sit-ins, this one at a Woolworth's lunch counter. On February 1, 1960, a group of black students sat at whites-only lunch counters and refused to move until served. Instead of being served, many were arrested. The news of the students' protest spread like wildfire across the South, and other students quickly followed their example. Sit-ins in Rock Hill, South Carolina, and Nashville, Tennessee, generated even more excitement.

By the end of the month, thirty-one sit-in campaigns had taken place in eight Southern states. King admired the students' courage. In a speech to students in Durham, North Carolina, he urged them to "fill up the jails." By April, sit-ins had become so widespread that students from all over the South held a conference to discuss their protests.

King's efforts to encourage the students' protests were hindered when he became the subject of more harassment from white authorities. When King moved to Atlanta from Alabama, the state of Alabama accused him of not paying enough income taxes. Not only was it possible that King would be put in jail for many years, but if his followers believed the charges, his reputation would be ruined. Like Daddy King, he had always kept careful financial records. He felt sure that the charges had been made up in order to destroy him, but still he had to prove his innocence.

King felt discouraged. Not sure that he could appear in public, he canceled appearances in Chicago and California. When he thought it over, however, he decided that he could not give up on the fight before it had begun. Giving in to the pressures of the tax charges would be like giving in to segregation. He rescheduled his speeches. In May 1960, King became the first person in Alabama to be tried by the state government for criminal tax evasion. He won the case, but there was no denying that the arrest had upset him deeply.

Putting that battle behind him, King searched for a way to become more directly involved in the protests for civil rights. Though Atlanta students asked him to participate in sit-ins with them, King felt that the protests belonged to the students and that his participation might overshadow their efforts. The students persisted, contacting King several times to request that he speak or sit with them in their protests. Finally, he agreed. On October 19, 1960, King joined the students at a downtown lunch counter and, as expected, their protest landed them in jail. King and the students spent four days behind bars before the students were released. King thought he would go free, too, but instead he was detained.

Officials from another county in Georgia claimed that King had violated probation from an earlier offense. Once, King had been stopped by police while driving with a white woman; this was yet another form of harassment. When the officer discovered that King's driver's license had expired, King was fined and put on a year's probation. With his arrest at the sit-in, King had violated his probation.

White authorities thus had the power to send King to jail for more than just an overnight stay. He was transferred from Atlanta to Dekalb County, a few miles away, for a hearing. A crowd of students gathered outside to watch as King emerged from the jail for the trip to the courthouse, guarded by two detectives and wearing handcuffs and leg and arm shackles. Even though the traffic violation was not serious, because King had violated probation, the judge had the latitude to sentence him to four months' hard labor.

The judge allowed Coretta and King's sister, Christine, to visit King for a few moments after the trial. King had been in jail for six days and looked tired. There was a chance that he could be hurt, or even killed, while serving his time in prison. Coretta, six months pregnant with their third child, cried when he spoke to her. When King asked her to be strong for him, Coretta cried even harder.

When Coretta and Martin parted, she resolved that something must be done to get him out of jail. This was an election year. King had endorsed neither the Democratic candidate, Massachusetts Senator John

F. Kennedy, nor the Republican, Vice-President Richard M. Nixon. He did not want to owe anyone any favors, and so he had decided to remain neutral. Still, Coretta frantically wanted to help her husband. Calling someone involved with the Kennedy campaign, she asked for help. The campaign worker convinced Kennedy to call Coretta to comfort her, just to let her know that he sympathized with her family. Though they talked for only a few minutes, news of the phone call spread quickly, and even appeared in a small article in *The New York Times*. John Kennedy's brother, Robert, head of the campaign, also intervened. He called the judge in charge of King's case and encouraged his release. On October 28, after nine days in jail, King left the prison and returned to Atlanta.

King was grateful for the Kennedys' help. His experience at the maximum-security prison had been a "test of faith," he said. As he wrote in his first letter to Coretta from jail, "This is the cross that we must bear for the freedom of our people." King did not endorse Kennedy directly, but Kennedy's campaign workers distributed a pamphlet throughout the black community that helped seal the election for him. The "blue bomb," as the pamphlet came to be known, quoted King's thanks to Kennedy for his help. Two million copies were printed and distributed to 10,000 churches. On Election Day, Kennedy received 75 percent of the black vote.

King was eager to work on civil-rights issues with the new president. Kennedy certainly seemed more receptive to the needs of black Americans than Eisenhower had been. The Kennedy Administration thought the best way to win equal rights was to fight for voter registration through enforcement of the nation's voting laws. King met with Kennedy shortly after the election in 1961 to discuss the president's ideas. While King thought Kennedy had good intentions, he was frustrated that the president was not willing to speak out immediately on the racial struggle.

The Kennedy administration soon became preoccupied with events in Cuba. Kennedy felt that Communist Cuba, situated so close to the U.S. mainland, posed a security threat to the nation. In April 1961, a Cuban force trained and armed by the United States tried to overthrow Fidel Castro's Communist government. However, the invasion at Cuba's Bay of Pigs was a failure, with Cuba capturing about 1,000 soldiers. News reports focused on Kennedy and his actions there rather than on the domestic crisis of civil rights.

Nonetheless, some progress was made. In May 1961, the Congress of Racial Equality decided to test Supreme Court rulings that declared that segregation on interstate buses and in bus terminals was unconstitutional. CORE sent black "Freedom Riders" on buses traveling across state lines and through the heart of the segregated South, from Washington to New Orleans, to see if the states would abide by the federal rulings.

When the first bus reached Rock Hill, South Carolina, angry whites punched a black student trying to enter the whites-only waiting room at the station. Still, the ride continued, arriving on May 13 in Atlanta, where riders met King for dinner. King, who had just been in Montgomery, Alabama, at an SCLC board meeting, warned students that tensions there were high. Alabama knew the Freedom Riders were coming and might meet them with violence.

King's worries were confirmed the next day. As the bus left Anniston, Alabama, the first stop in the state, a mob carrying bricks, pipes, and knives met the Freedom Riders at the station. The riders did not leave the bus, and the police avoided violence by ushering them out of town. However, about 200 men in fifty cars followed the bus on the highway. One of the bus's tires had been slashed at the station, and the driver was forced to pull over. When he did, the men surrounded the bus, smashed its windows, and threw a fire bomb inside, injuring many of the protesters. A photographer's picture of the burning bus brought national and international attention to the Freedom Riders when it appeared in newspapers the following day. America, and the White House, began to awaken to the nightmare of racial prejudice.

A second bus with Freedom Riders on board arrived in Anniston an hour later. The mob did not hurt them when they entered the station and got off the bus, but when they reboarded the bus, some white segregationists got on after them. They beat two of the white Freedom Riders and called them "nigger lovers." Violence continued when the bus arrived in Birmingham, Alabama, where the Ku Klux Klan gave the riders a merciless beating. The city's police chief, Eugene "Bull" Connor, allowed the mob to club, chain, and kick the riders for fifteen minutes before moving in to stop the violence.

All of this occurred with television network news

reporters looking on. By now, Attorney General Robert Kennedy was concerned for the Freedom Riders, and he sent a representative from his office to help them. The riders were determined to continue their trip to Montgomery, but Bobby Kennedy talked them out of it, arguing that the riders could not count on receiving protection from the state's governor, who supported segregation. They would have to fly out of Birmingham. At the airport, every time the flight carrying the Freedom Riders was announced, a bomb threat held the plane on the ground. Finally, without any announcement or warning, the plane took off for New Orleans.

Other students decided to go to Birmingham and continue the trip where the first riders had been stopped. Somehow, it was felt, a bus must make it to Montgomery. Two days after the first students had arrived in Birmingham, another group arrived at the station, only to be arrested by police chief Bull Connor. Taking them into "protective custody," Connor drove the students to the state line that night. He thought that by getting the riders out of Alabama he could end the protest. But the students returned to Birmingham to continue their journey.

From Washington, Bobby Kennedy instructed his representative in Birmingham to arrange for protection for the riders. After much discussion, the governor grudgingly promised that the Freedom Riders could travel safely to Montgomery. A bus left for Montgomery on May 20, six days after the first bus had entered Alabama.

At home in Atlanta, King watched television reports of the riders' reception in Montgomery. No police protected the students, as the governor had promised they would. An angry group of men emerged from the station and beat the riders, the reporters covering the event, and even the attorney general's representative. Ten minutes later, Montgomery's police commissioner, L.B. Sullivan, arrived with Alabama Attorney General MacDonald Gallion. They served the riders with a court order stating that their ride was illegal because it could lead to violence.

The next day, King flew to Montgomery in a show of support for the riders. While he led a mass meeting in Abernathy's church that night, a mob of angry whites overturned a car and set it on fire. The mob battered the church door and threw rocks through its windows. As the night wore on, U.S. marshals arrived with tear gas to disperse the angry crowd, followed by Alabama National Guardsmen. Although authorities were supposed to protect the protesters, National Guardsmen actually threatened students and supporters with their bayonets!

Eventually, Attorney General Robert Kennedy stepped in to force the cooperation of the National Guardsmen. After a heated argument, Alabama's governor agreed that the people at the mass meeting would have the Guard's protection — all except for King. The governor wanted to make the point with Kennedy that, for political reasons, he, the governor, could not offer to protect the most hated black man in Alabama. Luckily, King was not hurt that night.

While the riders struggled through the summer of 1961, King traveled all over the country raising money for them. It was tiring work, and the riders continued to meet with opposition. But by late fall their efforts were finally rewarded. The Interstate Commerce Commission (ICC) broadened earlier rulings to outlaw segregation not only on interstate buses but in the bus stations served by those buses. These new regulations took effect on November 1.

During 1961, King also conducted what he called "People-to-People" tours to promote voter registration. Yet the harder King worked, the more the SCLC seemed to falter, even on the heels of the successful Freedom Rides. The SCLC needed funds badly. King appealed to the powerful National Baptist Convention for support, but was refused; although the church agreed with King's goals, it did not agree with the tactics he was using to attain them.

Another serious blow came when King was invited to meet privately with President Kennedy. King thought this might be an opportunity to make some headway with civil-rights legislation, but instead the President met him with surprising and shocking news. J. Edgar Hoover, the director of the FBI, believed that Stanley Levison, one of King's top aides, was a Communist and Soviet spy. At that time, when fear of Communist influence in the United States was still widespread, this was a serious accusation. It was true that Levison had been a member of the Communist Party, but King could not believe that his friend was a spy. Levison was never officially tried for spying, but King was disheartened by the president's news.

Despite his disappointment, King was soon provided with a chance to make another vocal and well-publicized stand — this time with protesters in Albany,

Georgia. In November 1961, three black students were arrested for sitting in the white section of Albany's bus station. Other arrests followed, as more protesters tested the limits of Albany's segregation laws. The Student Nonviolent Coordinating Committee soon organized a Freedom Ride into Albany's train station, where Police Chief Laurie Pritchett arrested everyone involved. The next morning, 400 people marched from Shiloh Baptist Church toward city hall to protest the arrests, and Chief Pritchett had many of *them* arrested, too. *The New York Times* reported that, by December 13, 267 blacks had been arrested.

During this time, King's exposure was increasing. In October the BBC in London had interviewed him on a program about racism in America. In December, six weeks into the Albany movement, King went to Florida to address a national meeting of the American Federation of Labor-Congress of Industrial Organizations (AFL-CIO), a powerful labor union. He appealed to the group for support, asking them to recognize that issues affecting working-class blacks also affected working-class whites. King's speech was a success. He had won the support of the powerful political group and received important attention from the news media because of it.

As he traveled, he watched the events in Albany with interest. The SNCC had started a boycott of downtown stores in addition to buses. So far the group's actions had been carried out successfully, but leaders there wanted to bring in some more powerful and experienced help. By the time Albany leaders contacted King, the National Guard had been called in and reports of beatings were coming from the increasingly crowded jail.

An enthusiastic crowd welcomed King to Albany on December 15, 1961. The mass meeting he addressed that night spilled over into two churches. King moved the audience with a protest speech that began slowly with a history of the race struggle. He brought his speech around to Albany and expressed his support for the marchers' efforts. King picked up the pace of his speech as he asked "How long?" they would have to suffer. "Not long" was his own reply. He continued in a rising series of "How long? . . .Not long" questions that ended with "But we shall overcome." At the end of his speech, the emotional crowd broke into a thunderous version of "We Shall Overcome."

A march on city hall was planned for the next day. Linking arms with William Anderson, one of the city's black leaders, King led Abernathy and 265 others toward city hall. Police stopped them and arrested them for parading without a permit. As the protesters marched to jail they again sang "We Shall Overcome." This and other protest songs, such as "Oh Freedom" and "This Little Light of Mine," were characteristic of the Albany movement and spread to other demonstrations throughout the South. When King arrived in jail that day, he joined 750 other protesters. He hoped that this would be his chance to fill the jails.

But his hopes were dashed by conflict and competition among different factions within the Albany movement. Despite their having asked him to participate, some SNCC leaders resented King's appearance there. They accused him of grandstanding and trying to take over their movement. The NAACP, too, did not seem pleased with events in Albany. It criticized the SNCC's actions, which challenged the law through protests rather than by working within the system, through the courts.

Negotiations between the city and black protesters did not go well, perhaps in part because of this discord. Officials released King and demanded that he leave Albany until his sentencing in July. Under fire from the other black groups working in Albany, and unable to budge city officials, King agreed to leave. The city further undermined the protest by releasing everyone who had been arrested. This ruined the movement's efforts to show the absurdity of laws that, if enforced, could land so many people in jail. King left Albany without having won the fight. The papers did not respond well to King's role in Albany. The New York *Herald Tribune*, for one, called the experience "a devastating loss of face" for him.

When King and Abernathy returned to Albany for sentencing in July 1962, they initiated more nonviolent protests, and they went to jail two more times. King saw little of his family during this period. On the rare occasions he was at home, King easily relaxed with six-year-old Yoki, four-year-old Marty, and their third child, one-year-old Dexter. King played with them, telling them jokes and tickling them. Unlike his own father, he encouraged them to express their ideas. Children needed guidance, he believed, but not too firm a grip. Like his father, he tried to shield them from the pains of segregation and discrimination. Yet

77

no amount of protection could completely shut out the outside white world. On one occasion, King had the painful task of explaining to Yoki that she could not go to a whites-only amusement park simply because of the color of her skin.

While King was in jail in Albany that August, Yoki cried for her father. When Coretta explained that he was imprisoned so that she could go to the amusement park one day, Yoki exclaimed that he should stay there until she could! On August 5, Coretta brought all the children to the Albany jail to see their father. Seeing his children lifted King's spirits. In trying times, his family offered encouragement.

A few days after the family visit, King and Abernathy were released from jail. By then, Albany officials had virtually shut down the city. The pools were closed. The parks were closed. Even the library was closed so no blacks would be tempted to try to take out a book in order to challenge the segregation laws. In a last attempt to make the Albany movement succeed, King called on preachers from around the country to join him in another march there. Seventy-four joined him, but the event drew little attention.

Though King viewed Albany as a failure, he had come that much closer to realizing his dream of nonviolent protest. He and the marchers had nearly filled the jails, even if they had not succeeded in changing local segregation policies. Just as King realized on his return from India that he needed to devote all his time to the movement, he now realized that he needed to rethink his strategy. The Albany movement had failed for lack of a clear plan and dissension among the organizations involved. Frustrating their efforts, Chief Pritchett met nonviolent protest with nonviolent law enforcement. King was determined that his next move would combine the philosophy he wanted to practice and the political lessons he had learned in Albany.

7

March Through Birmingham

WITH THE LESSONS of Albany behind him, King worked at developing a comprehensive plan for realizing his dream of effective non-violent protest. All over the country, the struggle for civil rights was heating up. In Mississippi, a young black man named James H. Meredith wanted to attend the University of Mississippi at Oxford, despite the insistence of state governor Ross Barnett that "Ole Miss," as the school was known, would always be segregated.

Also in Mississippi, Bob Moses of the SNCC was working on registering blacks to vote. He met with violent resistance from whites. Tensions were so high that black churches were burned, and shots were fired into the homes of SNCC workers in Ruleville. President Kennedy, once reluctant to speak out directly on civil rights, attacked the shootings as "cowardly as well as outrageous." He said he could not understand why some people had to react with such violence just because blacks wanted to vote.

It was in this climate that King and Fred Shuttlesworth, leader of the Alabama Christian Movement for Human Rights (an ally of the SCLC), talked about desegregating the Alabama city of Birmingham. The blacks of Birmingham suffered under some of the South's strictest segregation laws. The city's police commissioner, Bull Connor, had illustrated his unwillingness to comply with desegregation policies in 1961 when he allowed crowds to beat the Freedom Riders. In 1962, Birmingham voted to reorganize its government, and King saw this as an opportunity for him to move his civil-rights movement into the city. Birmingham was a good site for a second reason: The NAACP was not active there (it had been outlawed in the state of Alabama) and the SNCC did not have any campaigns there. King would not risk the same intramovement quarrels that had divided the protest in Albany.

After the embarrassments at Albany, King wanted to develop a more complete nonviolent protest plan. He and Shuttlesworth planned to confront the city's segregation laws by attacking one of its most vulnerable points — its economy. By staging sit-ins and boycotts of downtown department stores, they hoped to draw city officials into open conflict. As King put it, he wanted to draw the enemy out and make them commit their wrongs in the open. They called the plan "Project C" for "Confrontation Birmingham."

While King planned his Birmingham campaign, in late 1962 and early 1963, the FBI continued to harass him by attacking those closest to him. Before going to Birmingham, the FBI placed an article in newspapers about one of King's associates, Jack O'Dell, one of the

81

most effective fund raisers in the SCLC's New York office. The article said that O'Dell was a Communist. The FBI's director, J. Edgar Hoover, believed that in the interests of national security his agency could go to almost any lengths to obtain information on suspected Communists. The FBI thus received permission from the attorney general's office to place wiretaps on people's telephones, and "bugs," or electronic surveillance devices, in their homes.

King found the charges against O'Dell hard to believe, but he had to be cautious about bad publicity if he wanted the Birmingham movement to succeed. He carefully distanced himself from O'Dell and pretended he did not know him. (Secretly, however, O'Dell continued to work with King on Project C.) To make matters worse for King, an article appeared in *The New York Times* with a headline saying that King thought the FBI favored segregationists in Albany, Georgia. This made Hoover furious, and he increased the FBI's investigation of King and his closest advisers.

Wary of the FBI, King wanted to keep the Birmingham plan a secret until it began. The group used code names on the phone, just in case the FBI had tapped them. After months of planning and preparation, Project C was revealed to the hand-picked circle of King's men who would carry it out.

First, small sit-ins and nightly mass meetings would be held to build support and make the city aware of the desegregation demands. Once the first step was complete, downtown businesses would be boycotted and larger demonstrations would be staged. Third, the protesters would hold mass marches to support the boycott and fill the jails. Last, if necessary they would ask for outside help to draw more attention to the protest and fill the city's jails with even more people. King's supporters assured him that they would have enough money for the venture, and promised they could win over Birmingham's black leaders in any difficult situation. Still, King warned colleagues that some of them might not live through the experience.

Late in February 1963, as King prepared for Birmingham, the issue of civil rights received renewed attention from President Kennedy. Kennedy, who believed civil-rights legislation would not pass in Congress, had always maintained that the biggest strides could be made by appointing blacks to government positions and enforcing existing civil-rights decisions through the attorney general's office. Kennedy responded to pressure from all sides and introduced a voting-rights bill. Unfortunately, the bill was hastily written and poorly organized, and never made it through Congress. Even so, the president's willingness to support legislation encouraged civil rights leaders.

King's sermons just before Birmingham revealed his determination to battle racism with nonviolence. As he spoke to the Ebenezer congregation about his hopes for the future, he preached that the sins of the private person could be converted through the good work of the public person. King prepared himself to face his opponents — not enemies — in Birmingham. He warned against the easiest evil of all, the sin against brotherhood.

On March 28, 1963, King's fourth child, Bernice,

was born. When King brought Coretta and the new baby home from the hospital a few days later, he finally felt fully prepared for Birmingham. King felt sure his support network was in place. That same day, April 2, as Coretta was settling in at home to take care of the newest member of the family, King arrived at Birmingham's Gaston Motel, the movement's headquarters.

On April 3, SCLC executive director Wyatt Tee Walker called between 250 and 350 people to gather at a mass meeting in the church where A.D. King, Martin's brother, was pastor. There, SCLC leaders distributed their "Birmingham Manifesto," which outlined the goals of Project C and openly declared that they would protest to fight segregation. The sit-ins began. When store owners undermined the sit-ins by simply closing down their stores, the SCLC countered with mass demonstrations. The first one, led by Fred Shuttlesworth on April 6, landed forty people in jail.

Meanwhile, Police Commissioner Connor obtained an injunction from a state judge ordering 133 people, including King, not to demonstrate in Birmingham. On April 12, King and Abernathy defied the order and led fifty people to jail. King was nervous about the move because he knew they already were running out of bail money. Even so, he said, "I have to make a faith act." As the marchers made their way toward Bull Connor's barricades, hundreds more joined in. When the march reached the police, King, Abernathy, and fifty-two others quickly disappeared into police vans and were herded off to jail.

King was thrown into solitary confinement. He was

not allowed to make a phone call or talk to a lawyer, and he had to sleep on a bed of metal slats with no mattress. On Monday, April 15, King's lawyer, Clarence Jones, was allowed to visit him. Jones told King that Harry Belafonte was raising bail money. He was also able to smuggle newspapers in to King.

But press coverage of the demonstrations did not lean in the movement's favor at first. King learned that both sides, black and white, criticized him for stirring up trouble that could ruin the small steps the city had already taken for the rights of its black citizens. The press pointed out that the new city government had barely had a chance before King stepped in. The reaction of the white pastors of Birmingham particularly irked King. They said the protest was "unwise and untimely," and called for an end to King's civil disobedience on religious grounds. The clergymen argued that "such actions as incite hatred and violence, however technically peaceful those actions may be, have not contributed to the resolution of our local problems."

When Jones returned to the jail the next day, he discovered that King had begun writing a long letter addressed to the clergymen. He wrote on the newspaper, filling up every margin and corner he could find, drawing arrows and loops from the end of one phrase to the beginning of the next. King told Jones he wasn't finished and asked for more paper.

This *Letter from a Birmingham Jail*, as King's article became known, was published in June 1963, both as excerpts in the *New York Post* and as a pamphlet distributed by a religious group called the American Friends Service Committee. However, its passionate explanation of the reasons for nonviolent resistance were clouded by the events surrounding King in Birmingham. It was only later that the *Letter* became a cornerstone of civil-rights literature.

In it, King described the necessity of nonviolent resistance — and the reasons why that resistance had to happen *now*. Why did King choose Birmingham? "Injustice anywhere is a threat to justice everywhere," he wrote. "We are . . .tied in a single garment of destiny. Whatever affects one directly affects all indirectly."

King pointed out that there had been black slaves in America for more than 300 years. Time after time, promises from whites to end discrimination were broken. Could blacks wait any longer to right these wrongs? Did waiting ever produce progress? He described the emotions blacks felt that made "now" the time for freedom. He described the history of lynchings, of beatings, of poverty, of having one's first name be "nigger" and one's middle name be "boy."

"There comes a time," King went on, "when the cup of endurance runs over, and men are no longer willing to be plunged into an abyss of injustice where they experience the blackness of corroding despair. I hope . . .you can understand our legitimate and unavoidable impatience."

King also explained the difference between just and unjust laws. How could anyone, morally and in good conscience, abide by an unjust law? He pointed out that "it was 'illegal' to aid and comfort a Jew in Hitler's Germany. But I am sure that if I had lived in Germany during that time I would have aided and comforted my Jewish brothers even though it was illegal." Finally, King criticized liberal whites who claimed to support rights for blacks yet failed to aid the movement: "Shallow understanding from people of goodwill is more frustrating than absolute misunderstanding from people of ill will. Lukewarm acceptance is much more bewildering than outright rejection." King closed his letter with his criticisms of the church. Many clergymen openly attacked his efforts, while others claimed to support him but did not urge their congregations to follow integration rulings. He called on them to meet with him as a brother in their faith, not as a civil-rights leader.

On April 20, nine days after having been imprisoned, King was released. During his time in jail, another civil-rights leader, James Bevel, had trained many Birmingham grade-school and high-school students in nonviolent protest techniques. The children had come to him wanting to join their movement. SCLC leaders were not sure they should risk the possibility of children going to jail. King worried that they might be hurt, but he also knew their lives could be much worse under segregation. In the end, King and Bevel decided to let the children march.

On May 2, 1963, the first children set off from Birmingham's Sixteenth Street Baptist Church. At first, fifty children emerged from the church, only to be led into vans by police. Then another line of children came out of the church, and another. Soon there were more teenagers leaving the church than could fit inside police vans. By 4:00 P.M., about 1,000 youths had participated in the march through Birmingham. Most of them spent the night in Birmingham's jail, as

All too often, black people who protested against racial discrimination were jailed by order of the law. King is shown here in Florida in 1962, one of the many times he was locked up after leading demonstrations to promote the cause of racial equality and integration.

many as seventy-five jammed into a cell designed for eight people.

The next day, the children's march resumed. Bull Connor called out the fire department to stop them, and when the children reached the barricades they sang "Freedom" to the tune of "Amen." Officials ordered them to disperse, but the children continued singing. A few moments later, firemen turned powerful water hoses on them. Most of the children scattered, but a few stood their ground. One girl was swept down the street from the force of the water, her limbs flailing helplessly, her body rolling like a tumbleweed in a high wind.

More children came out of the Sixteenth Street Baptist Church. Overwhelmed by the numbers of marchers, the police could not hold them, so they released eight "K-9" units — teams of dogs — on the children. That night, America's television news programs broadcast pictures of the vicious attack on the marchers. One officer held a boy by the shirt while he let his dog bite into the child's stomach. The sight outraged viewers, and resulted in greater support for the civil-rights movement. In the White House, President Kennedy responded immediately, sending the assistant attorney general, Burke Marshall, to Birmingham.

At the movement's mass meetings King encouraged more and more children to march for freedom. On Saturday, marchers surprised the police. The police had set up barriers to keep protesters out of downtown Birmingham, but many children managed to get around the barriers, and they gathered outside City Hall. Bull Connor, who did not like being outmaneuvered, soon ordered any groups of blacks on the streets arrested. He then sealed off the entrances to the churches where the children gathered to march, so they could not leave. Adults standing by began throwing rocks at the officers. King's men were able to calm the crowd, but tensions were running high.

The next day, Sunday, planned as a day of rest, instead saw continued protest activity, as protest leaders wanted to keep up the momentum and walk again. About 2,000 children marched, and again they encountered city firemen. Bull Connor was there, too. At the blockade, the marchers knelt to pray. After a few moments, Charles Billups, a Birmingham minister, stood up and challenged the firemen to go ahead and turn on the hoses. They would stand there, said Billups, until they died. "Turn them on," Bull Connor barked in reply. The firemen looked at the children and then at Connor, but they did nothing. Even when Connor shouted at them again to turn their hoses on the protesters, they could not obey the order.

The campaign continued. Monday, May 6, was the day when more nonviolent protesters — 1,000 — were arrested than on any day in American history. Ten people per minute marched to jail for almost two hours. The next day, 3,000 protesters eluded police blockades once again and filled Birmingham's business district. With such a huge crowd, King worried that violence would erupt. Sure enough, by three o'clock the firemen's hoses were being answered with rocks.

Events escalated until President Kennedy intervened, demanding that the two sides reach a settlement. On Friday, May 10, with the U.S. assistant district attorney mediating, Birmingham and its black citizens reached an agreement. The settlement said that sitting rooms, rest rooms, water fountains, and lunch counters would all be integrated within the month and that a biracial committee would be formed to hammer out any more differences between whites and blacks.

King's campaign had worked! Even as the announcement of the agreement was being made, however, Birmingham's mayor-elect, Albert Boutwell, blustered that he would not follow through on it. The settlement also angered members of the Ku Klux Klan. A bomb went off at A.D. King's home in Birmingham, and another exploded at the Gaston Motel on Saturday. In retaliation blacks began throwing rocks and shouting for revenge. The riot raged all through the night of May 11. The governor of Alabama sent in state troopers, who provoked more violence from blacks. Before it was over, President Kennedy had to order federal troops to move into Birmingham. The troops quieted the city — for the time being.

When King finally left Birmingham to continue his work, he had little notion of how the experience would change his life. He was devastated by this outburst of violence. To him, it was a crushing blow to the success of the Birmingham movement. Still, King was sure that Birmingham had brought the cause of civil rights to the attention of more Americans than he had been able to reach before. He deeply regretted the violence that had resulted, but there was no denying that his efforts to stage a nonviolent protest had resulted in gains for the city's blacks. The children's march to the jail had had more impact than any action he had staged so far in his career. He did not imagine that the protest would spark such widespread social change or so profoundly affect his own career.

8

I Have a Dream

BIRMINGHAM HAD A powerful impact on the nation. With images of children being bitten by police dogs and pushed against walls with water hoses fresh in their minds, Americans finally began to view civil rights as an important issue. In June 1963, President Kennedy agreed to sponsor a new civil-rights bill. King and his SCLC followers did not want to lose the momentum begun in Birmingham. They believed Congress needed a push to act immediately on the proposed bill.

King's fellow civil-rights leaders, Bayard Rustin and A. Philip Randolph, began planning a march on Washington for August 1963. The year marked the one-hundredth anniversary of President Lincoln's Emancipation Proclamation, which freed black slaves, and King wanted Kennedy to issue a second proclamation. Through the combined efforts of civil-rights groups — including the NAACP, the Brotherhood of Sleeping Car Porters, CORE, and King's own SCLC — the march would surpass black leaders' highest hopes for what would be the largest civil-rights demonstration in American history.

Organizers had little more than three months to plan the event that they expected would draw some 100,000 people. The march would end in a rally at which black leaders would speak. Though King, who was at the time thirty-four years old, did not play a major role in planning the march, he commanded the attention of black and white leaders alike and was the movement's most popular figure. He was to be the featured speaker at the rally, speaking last.

In June, when the march was in its early planning stages, Kennedy met with King and other black leaders. The mood of the meeting was optimistic. However, the president objected to the march, arguing that it might anger legislators rather than convince them to vote for the civil-rights bill. After the meeting, Kennedy led King into the White House rose garden to speak with him privately. King felt honored to be taken into the President's confidence, but his mood changed when the President began to speak.

The FBI believed that Stanley Levison had not ended his involvement with the Communist Party, and it maintained its earlier charge that Levison was a Soviet spy. Since King was now so close to the President, he could not associate with someone as "dangerous" as Levison. Kennedy told King he must break all ties with his friend. The President also reminded King that he should end his relationship with Jack O'Dell, who continued to work for King at the SCLC's New York office.

King could not believe his ears. He asked the president for evidence, but Kennedy would not tell him how the FBI knew these things. (In fact, the FBI would not even reveal its sources to the President; he had had to take the organization's word for it that the charges were true.)

When King left the White House he didn't know whether he should laugh or be upset. The charges against Levison seemed ridiculous. Levison was one of King's closest friends; he had been there throughout the Birmingham campaign. King would never believe the charge that Levison was a spy, but to protect the movement he would have to respond to the President's warning. King disliked having to discipline his staff for any reason, but now he faced telling two of his closest associates that they could not work with him anymore.

Difficult as it was, King met first with O'Dell to tell him the news, explaining that complete separation would be the only way to keep the movement strong. King was less willing to fire Levison, and perhaps his friend recognized this. In the end, Levison saved King from having to ask him to resign by leaving of his own accord. Knowing it would help the movement, the two men finally broke all ties.

The FBI was not the only source of trouble for King. He also came under fire from other activists fighting for black equality. One such leader was Malcolm X, whose approach to winning freedom from oppression for blacks differed from King's. Malcolm X believed that blacks should create their own powerful nation, free from the influence and oppression of whites. He advocated overthrowing white power and replacing it with black power. As far as he was concerned, King's nonviolent strategy only pacified blacks, making them victims of white oppression. Malcolm X encouraged blacks to fight discrimination with violence. Though King admired Malcolm X as a well-spoken leader, he could not support his violent tactics.

Despite his troubles, King's popularity increased. Throughout the summer of 1963 he traveled from city to city speaking about what had happened in Birmingham. He built support for the coming march, drawing crowds of 10,000, 20,000, and 25,000 people in some cities. Blacks across the country still held the image of Birmingham in their minds. They launched their own nonviolent conflicts in close to 900 cities. Spirits were high.

That summer King began to work on another book, *Why We Can't Wait*. As he explained in his *Letter from a Birmingham Jail*, King described the long history of events and conditions that made the struggle for freedom so important *now*. He wanted to finish the book before the march. But even though he took a three-week break from his speaking tour to devote himself to writing full-time, this proved to be too little time. As the date of the march approached, King put his book aside and turned his thoughts to the event that would remain fixed in people's minds for years to come as a high point of the black struggle for civil rights. (The book was published in 1964.)

Black leaders had worked hard to prepare for the march. As they arrived in Washington on August 27, the day before the march, the city hummed with preparations and anticipation. To cope with the enormous crowds, a large security force had been formed. Still, some worried that the crowd might riot. The city refused to sell alcohol, some store owners moved goods to warehouses in case of looting, and hospitals readied operating rooms in case violence broke out.

On the night before the march, King rushed to Washington from two last days of speech-making in other cities. He still needed to write his own speech for the rally. All the leaders wanted to present a unified voice that would not incite violence. Each chose his words carefully, knowing each had only eight minutes to talk. Abernathy and other close advisers stayed up all night long at the hotel as King wrote and rewrote. How could he say all he needed to in just eight minutes? He asked Abernathy and the others for suggestions. While they stood by faithfully to help him edit a phrase or find a new image, they told King to let the spirit move him. He would know what to say. Finally, as the sun began to rise over Washington, a typist began reproducing King's hand-written speech.

The hot August day drew thousands to Washington. They came by car, bus, plane, train, on roller skates, and by bicycle. They came in much greater numbers than had been predicted — anywhere from 250,000 to 500,000 people are estimated to have marched that day to the Lincoln Memorial.

In the morning, performers Joan Baez, Odetta, and Peter, Paul, and Mary inspired the crowd with protest songs at the Washington Monument. By 1:30, the crowd restlessly awaited the speakers, and soon the first one took the podium. Throughout the hot afternoon, they listened to speaker after speaker. Between speeches, singers Josephine Baker, Marian Anderson, and Mahalia Jackson roused the crowd with their songs. The crowd grew tired as the afternoon wore on, but their impatience grew into excited anticipation as Martin Luther King, Jr., stepped to the podium.

Applause filled the air for a full minute before King began to speak. The major television networks interrupted their programming to broadcast King's speech live. King began by recalling the man who had signed the Emancipation Proclamation. His clear, baritone voice filled the air as he went on to point out that America had not fulfilled the promise of true freedom for blacks. They were "still sadly crippled by the manacles of segregation and the chains of discrimination."

King relied on his notes, yet interacted with the crowd as if he were at a huge mass meeting. He called on the nation to remember that the Declaration of Independence and Constitution promised all people the right to life, liberty, and the pursuit of happiness. "It is obvious today that America has defaulted on this promissory note," King said. He likened it to America writing blacks a bad check, "a check which has come back marked 'insufficient funds.'" King built on this idea, saying that America's people believed the "bank of justice" could not be bankrupt. They were gathered in Washington today to cash that check. Echoing the theme of "freedom now," King cried, "*Now* is the time to make real the promises of democracy. *Now* is the time to rise from the dark and desolate valley of segregation to the sunlit path of racial justice." He cautioned Americans to demand payment for justice by nonviolent means. Hatred provided no answer to blacks' oppression, he said. He pointed out that whites had joined the movement, and many of them were at the rally that day.

Throughout the speech, the crowd responded with "Yes" and "Right on!" Toward the end of the speech, King was overcome with the moment and the large crowd's responsiveness. Abandoning his notes, he passionately began to share his dream.

"So I say to you, my friends, that even though we must face the difficulties of today and tomorrow, I still have a dream. It is a dream deeply rooted in the American dream that one day this nation will rise up and live out the true meaning of its creed — we hold these truths to be self-evident, that all men are created equal.

"I have a dream that one day on the red hills of Georgia, sons of former slaves and sons of former slave-owners will be able to sit down together at the table of brotherhood.

"I have a dream that one day, even the state of Mississippi, a desert state sweltering with the heat of injustice, sweltering with the heat of oppression, will be transformed into an oasis of freedom and justice.

"I have a dream my four little children will one day live in a nation where they will not be judged by the color of their skin but by the content of their character. I have a dream today!

"I have a dream that one day, down in Alabama, with its vicious racists, with its governor having his lips dripping with the words of interposition and nullification, that one day, right there in Alabama, little black boys and black girls will be able to join hands with little white boys and white girls as sisters and brothers. I have a dream today!

99

"I have a dream that one day every valley shall be exalted, every hill and mountain shall be made low, the rough places shall be made plain, and the crooked places will be made straight. . . . With this faith we will be able to hew out of the mountain of despair a stone of hope. With this faith we will be able to transform the jangling discords of our nation into a beautiful symphony of brotherhood."

By now the crowd swayed in rhythm with the cadence of his words. Someone said, "Dream some more." On the platform, people urged him on with "Tell it, doctor!" and "All right!"

King sent chills down the spines of his listeners when he recited the words to "My Country 'Tis of Thee": "From every mountainside let freedom ring." He built to his closing. "When we let freedom ring . . . we will be able to speed up that day when all of God's children, black men and white men, Jews and gentiles, Protestants and Catholics, will be able to join hands and sing in the words of the old Negro spiritual, 'Free at last! Free at Last! Thank God Almighty, we are free at last!'"

Thunderous applause met King as he stepped away from the podium. At home, millions of television viewers heard the cry of freedom from a man who had moved smaller audiences all over the nation. Watching on his set in the White House, President Kennedy commented on King's masterful technique as a speaker. When he shook his hand at a reception later in the afternoon, Kennedy echoed King's words, saying to him, "I have a dream."

But after the successful march, violence seemed to erupt everywhere. In Birmingham in September, a bomb exploded in the Sixteenth Street Baptist Church and killed four young girls. At the service King gave for the deceased, the high he had experienced in August quickly turned to the grim reality of violence. Violence went on to plague the city of Birmingham for weeks. By the end of September, King felt discouraged. The dream of nonviolence no longer seemed to work in Birmingham.

Then, on November, 22, 1963, King lost a strong ally in the struggle for civil rights. President Kennedy was assassinated while visiting Dallas, Texas. With the rest of the nation, King was devastated by the news. It seemed to him that if the President could not escape the violence of hatred, he could not escape it either. Now thirty-four years old, King grimly told Coretta that he did not think he would live beyond the age of forty.

9

March to Montgomery

IN HIS FIRST speech to Congress, the new president, Lyndon B. Johnson, urged legislators to pass Kennedy's Civil Rights Bill, saying it would be the best memorial they could give the slain president.

King, meanwhile, enjoyed more popularity than ever. In January 1964, he appeared on the cover of *Time* as its "Man of the Year." Some people now compared him to a modern-day messiah, and this troubled King. He was not a messiah, simply a man challenging the moral injustices of his time. He did not want fame. He simply wanted to do good work in the name of justice. King still traveled a lot delivering speeches, and his hectic schedule took its toll on him. He sometimes complained of stomachaches and had trouble sleeping.

Throughout 1964 new events distracted King from launching the same kind of campaign that had proved so successful in Birmingham. The SCLC's efforts on voting rights, which had been renewed following the failure of Kennedy's 1963 bill, continued to encounter resistance. Race riots broke out in St. Augustine, Florida, on May 28, 1964. The Klan lashed out when civil-rights activists there began demonstrations to desegregate public places and fight for voting rights. King pleaded with President Johnson to send in troops to stop the violence, but the White House treated the matter as a local concern and would not step in.

On May 31, King himself went to St. Augustine to join the protest, taking his six-year-old son, Marty, with him. King and Ralph Abernathy led marches and went to jail, protesting nonviolently amid the violence of whites who opposed desegregation. They hoped their nonviolent tactics would give them bargaining power, as it had in Birmingham and Montgomery. They made little progress until the beginning of July, when a judge finally ordered that a racially mixed committee start talks between St. Augustine's whites and blacks. Now King could leave the troubled city and return to his voting-rights campaign.

In July, the 1964 Civil Rights Act became law. Motels would now be desegregated, and discrimination in businesses and labor unions was outlawed. But the act fell short of the expectations of civil rights leaders in some areas, in particular because it ignored voting rights and housing for the poor. The faults in the Civil Rights Act pushed King and other leaders into action. That summer, the SNCC and CORE launched a "Freedom Summer" campaign, traveling throughout the South to convince blacks to register to vote. At the same time, King and the SCLC began a "People-to-People" tour. Their aim was to support the voter registration campaign by teaching black people to read; without that skill, blacks could not pass the test to register.

Resistance to these campaigns by racist whites was fierce and violent. In July 1964, three CORE volunteers working on the "Freedom Summer" campaign in Philadelphia, Mississippi, disappeared without a trace and were feared murdered. In a massive FBI manhunt, hundreds of FBI agents and Navy personnel conducted a dragnet, or search, of the town and surrounding swamps and woods. It wasn't until three weeks later that they found the bodies of the young men — one black and two whites — buried in a muddy hillside. Eighteen people were arrested in connection with the murders, including Philadelphia's Sheriff Rainey, his deputy, and other prominent white citizens from the area. Despite the seriousness of their crime, however, these men were treated as heroes by the local white community, and only seven of the orginal eighteen men arrested were convicted.

Violent crimes by whites who opposed equal rights for blacks continued. By the end of 1964, in Mississippi alone 6 blacks had been killed, 80 beaten, and 1,000 arrested, and 68 black churches and homes had been burned or bombed. Still, blacks would not give up the "Freedom Summer" campaign, or their fight for equality in other areas. Across the country, blacks protested unfair living conditions during the long, hot summer of 1964. Riots broke out in northern cities such as Newark, New Jersey, Chicago, Illinois, and New York. King worked double duty: on the People-to-People campaign in the South, and urging blacks in the North not to resort to violence. Tensions were high, and this work took all of King's energy.

By the fall, an exhausted King took precious time out for a rest. Waking up after his first full night's sleep in weeks, he was greeted with heartening news: He had been nominated to receive the Nobel Peace Prize! The Nobel Prize is an international award given each year to people who have contributed greatly to work in the sciences, literature, the cause of peace, and other fields. In December, Martin and Coretta, along with King's parents, his brother, A.D., and the Abernathys flew to Norway for the Nobel ceremony. At the age of thirty-five, King became the youngest man ever to receive the coveted prize for peace.

Returning to America, King eagerly dove back into his work for voting rights. In January 1965, he and his friends began a campaign in Selma, Alabama, which they called "Project Alabama." Activists in Selma had already started their own campaign in 1964, attracting strong white opposition. As in Birmingham, Selma's officials were opposed to desegregation. Furthermore, the state's governor, George Wallace, had just won an election largely by vowing never to allow integration in Alabama's schools. King knew the struggle there would not be easy.

On the second day of the protest, Selma's Sheriff Jim Clark began arresting demonstrators who marched on the courthouse. But the protesters merely intensified the pressure on the city and continued to march. State troopers were called to the city, but that did not stop King and Abernathy from leading a protest that put them and 250 others in jail. While in jail, their staff continued demonstrating. By the time King was bailed out, 3,000 people had marched to Selma's jail.

The massive demonstrations drew the important camera crews and reporters needed to bring national attention to the movement. Although President Johnson became increasingly concerned about the events in Selma, when King flew to Washington hoping to meet with him, he was refused. After some discussion and maneuvering, King did meet with the president, but Johnson made no real commitment to help Project Alabama.

Shortly after King's return to Selma, a black man was killed following a march in a nearby town. The killing led King to step up the protest. He planned to march from Selma to the state capital in Montgomery and demand action from Governor Wallace. Wallace tried to stop the protesters, but on the morning of March 7, they began their march anyway. They expected they would be arrested for marching illegally. Instead, state troopers and men from the sheriff's office beat the protesters. Many were sent to hospitals as a result of the brutality.

Finally, sympathizers were moved to act. Protesters in Northern cities staged sympathy marches. King sent telegrams across the country asking clergymen to join the protest in Selma, and they came by the hundreds. They, too, were attacked, and one minister died, the second victim of the violence in Selma. But Governor Wallace would still not allow the march.

Throughout his time in Selma, King and President Johnson met periodically to discuss events there. On March 15, the president at last took action, introduc-

King and his wife, Coretta, at a community salute held in 1964 in honor of King's winning the Nobel Prize for peace. At age 35, King was the youngest man ever to win the peace prize. The Nobel is given to individuals for outstanding work in a variety of fields, including the sciences, literature, and humanitarian services.

ing a voting-rights bill. Johnson's televised speech before Congress echoed the sentiments King had expressed time and again. Johnson spoke out strongly for the bill, telling Congress that now was the time to grant blacks their full right to vote. "Their cause must be our cause, too," he said. "Because it's not just Negroes, but really it's all of us who must overcome the crippling legacy of bigotry and injustice." King was moved to tears when Johnson closed with the cry of the civil-rights movement: "And we *shall* overcome!"

Two days later, a federal judge ordered the state not to interfere with the march to Montgomery. For three days, King, Abernathy, Ralph Bunche of the United Nations, and Rabbi Abraham Heschel of the Jewish Theological Seminary of America led more than 3,000 marchers on the fifty-mile trek from Selma to Montgomery. State troopers who had so recently beat the protesters now led them out of the city. Police helicopters watched the scene from above, and troops at the side of the road protected the marchers along the route. Selma's angry whites watched as the marchers passed them as they left the city on March 21, 1965, but though some shouted insults, there was no violence.

Along the way, the marchers saw constant reminders of the reasons for their protest. A black church desperately needed a new roof and many of its windows were broken. Broken-down shacks testified to the poverty of many blacks.

On March 24, the marchers triumphantly entered Alabama's capital city. That night 10,000 people listened to celebrities such as Harry Belafonte, Joan

Baez, and writer James Baldwin at a rally. King spoke passionately to the crowd.

"What do you want?" he asked.

"Freedom!" they shouted.

"When do you want it?"

"*Now!*"

The demonstration in the heart of Southern segregationist territory filled civil-rights advocates with hope. King addressed the crowd with the same passion that had made his speech in Washington such a success the year before. He spoke to a crowd of both blacks and whites. More important, the crowd had traveled into the South to voice its demands for equal rights. King had returned to the city that launched him into the civil-rights struggle to a victory even more far-reaching than the bus-boycott triumph had been.

10

Free At Last

MANY VIEWED THE march to Montgomery as the movement's — and King's — finest demonstration. King wondered what he could do next to match such an inspirational and effective protest. It was with confidence that he began to look to other pressing issues concerning blacks. He continued to lobby Washington to pass a strong voting-rights bill, but during the spring of 1965, King also turned to the second item the 1964 Civil Rights Act ignored: poverty and housing.

During their travels around the world and in America, King and Coretta were deeply troubled by the sight of whole families devastated by poverty. The image of the poor in India still stuck in his mind. More recently, he had visited the ghettos of Northern cities where blacks lived in appalling conditions. King believed that poverty destroyed the souls of people as much as it destroyed their health and well-being. President Johnson had announced a "War on Poverty," but King did not think the government was acting quickly enough to help America's poor. King feared that the violence that had erupted in Northern cities during the summer of 1964 might be sparked again if he did not do something soon.

King first used his nonviolent tactics to attack poverty in Chicago. In what he called the Chicago Freedom Movement, he led marches into white neighborhoods to protest the pathetic conditions of black slums. But the campaign went slowly and incited violence from whites. On one march, King was hit in the head with a brick, but he was not seriously injured. By the spring of 1966, he still had not generated much interest in his war on poverty.

By this time, King's SCLC and other black groups had grown apart. The SNCC and CORE had grown impatient with the slow gains of the civil-rights movement. Some now advocated the revolutionary cry of "Black Power" over the SCLC's peaceful call for "Freedom Now." They had drifted away from King's ideas on nonviolence. In June 1966, King joined other black groups in a march to protest the attempted murder of James Meredith, the first black student to be enrolled at the University of Mississippi. But during the march, members of CORE and the SNCC argued with King about tactics. The march did not receive much attention and accomplished little.

King and his family moved to Chicago for the summer of 1966 to intensify the fight against widespread poverty there among blacks. His children were unhappy in Chicago, however, and King's nonviolent agitation fell apart when a riot broke out in mid-July. Shifting focus, King and the SCLC started "Operation

Breadbasket" in September. A young activist named Jesse Jackson was to oversee the project.

King reasoned that to find better housing, Chicago's blacks would have to earn more money. Operation Breadbasket was devised to pressure white-owned businesses to hire blacks. In the same way that they pressured white businesses to serve blacks at lunch counters in Birmingham, they would stage boycotts of businesses that refused to hire blacks.

By January 1967, King still had not realized any gains that resembled his successes in Montgomery, Birmingham, and Selma. "Black Power" was sweeping black youth up in its movement, while King's cry for nonviolent protest went unheeded. Chicago seemed to have defeated King. Discouraged and needing some time to rethink the direction his life should take, King left for the island of Jamaica to work on another book about the civil-rights movement, *Where Do We Go from Here?* Secluded in a cabin without a phone, King reviewed where the events of the past three years had brought him. He wrote about the movement's early successes and the new "Black Power" movement that advocated black unity and separatism. King agreed with the movement's thoughts on unity and strength, but he could not agree with the idea of separatism.

After he returned to the United States, King waged his war on poverty with renewed vigor. In August 1967, he told his aides that only a massive showing of civil disobedience in the nation's capital could draw the country's attention to the plight of the poor. They began their plans for a march to be held during the

UPI/Bettmann Newsphotos

King and Reverend Ralph Abernathy (reading newspaper), another prominent civil-rights activist, leading supporters in the famous Selma-to-Montgomery March of 1965. The demonstration was a milestone in the civil-rights movement because it brought the struggle to the heart of southern segregationist territory.

summer of 1968. As they began organizing the march, King traveled around the country looking for the support he had lost to a nation deeply divided over civil rights and U.S. involvement in a war in Vietnam. King spoke out against the war. His participation in a protest rally at the United Nations in New York City brought him criticism from all sides. Finding that he no longer drew the same enthusiastic crowds, he searched for a way to reignite the fire of his dream.

When James Lawson, who trained protesters for the SNCC, called from Memphis in February 1968, King sensed he might have found that spark. Lawson told him that Memphis's sanitation workers, most of whom were black, had organized to demand better wages and working conditions. The city had not recognized their demands, and the two sides were locked in a stalemate. The sanitation workers began a strike. When police attacked them, black groups rallied to support the workers.

King thought this sounded like the perfect campaign to build up recognition and support before the "Poor People's March" he was planning for Washington, D.C. The black community supported the organized labor efforts of the sanitation workers. The efforts of both groups might be combined very effectively. When King arrived in Memphis on March 18, an enthusiastic crowd of 17,000 met him. King had a good feeling about the campaign.

Still, there was some reason to worry. Shortly after King arrived in Memphis, an anonymous caller phoned a Memphis radio station warning that King would be killed. At the same time, Abernathy and other close associates noticed that King seemed to be preoccupied and depressed. King himself said that he thought he might be killed during the upcoming march to Washington. This was not just idle speculation; by 1968 the FBI had recorded fifty death threats against him.

Throughout the month of March, King flew in and out of Memphis to meet with the sanitation workers. A march there on March 28 resulted in violence, but King felt sure he could turn things around with his philosophy of nonviolence. He announced that he would return early in April to lead a nonviolent demonstration.

On April 3, King's flight from Atlanta to Memphis was delayed because of a bomb threat. He checked into Memphis's Lorraine Motel later that day, unnerved and slightly depressed over the continued threats on his life. King changed into his pajamas and tried to relax, but Abernathy called to say that 2,000 people wanted to hear him speak. King grudgingly agreed, dressed, and made his way to a local church.

There King spoke of the importance of living in the turbulent years of the civil-rights movement. He recalled that if he had sneezed when he had been stabbed in Harlem, he would not have seen the great social changes of the past few years. If God had given him a time to be on earth, King said, he would have chosen America in the twentieth century. He would not have missed his work with the civil-rights movement for anything. He went on to talk about the threats on his life. They didn't matter to him, he said, "Because I've been to the mountaintop. Like anybody I would like to live a long life. . . . But I'm not con-

cerned about that now. I just want to do God's will.
And He's allowed me to go up to the mountain. And
I've looked over. And I've *seen* the Promised Land.
And I may not get there with you. But I want you to
know tonight that we as a people will get to the Promised Land. . . . I have a dream this afternoon that the
brotherhood of man will become a reality. With this
faith, *I* will go out and carve a tunnel of hope from a
mountain of despair. . . . "

King's speech pulled him out of the depression he'd
been in. He was relaxed, and he had a good feeling
about what would happen in Memphis. The next day
he plunged into organizing the march. At around
5:30 in the evening, King and his aides prepared to go
to dinner. King stepped out onto the balcony of the
hotel and waited for everyone to get ready to leave.

Suddenly the sound of a gunshot ripped through
the air. King grabbed his neck as the force of the blast
knocked him onto his back. Abernathy, who reached
him first, thought he saw his friend trying to say
something with his eyes. The bullet had torn away
the right side of King's neck and face, and he was
soon saturated in a pool of blood. At the hospital,
doctors discovered that the bullet had ruptured arter-
ies and broken his spine. The doctors worked on his
wounds, but to no avail. An hour after he was shot,
Martin Luther King, Jr., was dead.

11

A Dream Deferred

WHEN JAMES EARL RAY assassinated Dr. Martin Luther King, Jr., on April 4, 1968, the entire nation mourned the loss. Three days later, on April 7, President Johnson declared a national day of mourning, and flags flew at half-staff. At his funeral in Atlanta on April 9, 800 people crowded the pews of Ebenezer Baptist Church, and between 60,000 and 100,000 more gathered outside. One hundred twenty million people watched on television as a mule-drawn casket led King on his last march, to Atlanta's South View Cemetery. There he was buried next to his beloved grandmother, Mama Williams. His gravestone bears a line from one of his favorite spirituals, and one he quoted often:

"Free At Last, Free At Last
Thank God Almighty
I'm Free At Last"

Coretta King once said that one night at a mass

meeting her husband stated, "If one day you find me sprawled and dead, I do not want you to retaliate with a single act of violence. I urge you to continue protesting with the same dignity and discipline you have shown so far." Nonetheless, at a time when racial tensions were high, and America was divided over the Vietnam War, King's death sparked a series of riots. One hundred ten cities across the nation reported riots during the day following his death. Thirty-nine people were killed and 75,000 federal troops and National Guardsmen were needed to restore calm to America's streets. The tragedy of the great nonviolent leader's death was heightened by this outpouring of violence.

Meanwhile, the nation waited anxiously for news about the FBI's manhunt for King's killer. After a two-month search covering the United States, Canada, and Europe, a drifter named James Earl Ray was captured in an airport in London, England. Ray had been in trouble with the law for most of his life. To catch him, the FBI spent $1,400,000 and deployed 3,014 agents in what was then its largest manhunt ever.

Since the assassination, there has been a good deal of speculation that Ray was part of a conspiracy, that he did not act alone in murdering King. For example, in St. Louis, where Ray lived, rewards of $20,000 to $50,000 were reportedly advertised. Some people believe Ray acted because of these offers, but this was never confirmed. Others point to the FBI's continued efforts to undermine King and say there was an FBI conspiracy to kill him. However, a congressional committee looking into the suspected plot found in 1978 that the FBI was not involved.

In any case, James Earl Ray was eventually found guilty of pulling the trigger and sentenced to ninety-nine years in prison. To this day, it is not known whether or not anyone else was involved.

Martin Luther King, Jr., was at the center of the civil rights movement throughout most of his life, and is considered by many to have been its most important leader. Even through the most difficult times, King persevered. There were times when violence erupted despite his efforts to maintain peace. But King never wavered from his course of nonviolent protest. His three books and the famous treatise, *Letter from a Birmingham Jail*, are still widely read. During the 1960s, more civil-rights legislation was passed than in any other decade. In 1964 he received international recognition for his pursuit of justice when he was awarded the Nobel Peace Prize. Today, the birthday of Martin Luther King, Jr., January 15, is a national holiday. His work began to reshape the attitudes of millions toward the rights of blacks. Clearly, the man who downplayed his influence and doubted his abilities as a leader made an incredible impact.

In his last Sunday sermon, delivered on March 31, 1968 in the National Cathedral of Washington, D.C., King spoke about "Remaining Awake Through a Great Revolution." He began with the story of Rip Van Winkle, the fictional figure who went up to a mountain and slept for twenty years. On his way to the mountain, he had passed a sign with a picture of King George III of England. When he awakened from his sleep, the sign had a picture of George Washington, the first President of the United States. He had slept through an entire revolution, through the founding of a nation.

King implored his audience not to sleep through the great social and political revolution he saw taking place in the world. It was everyone's responsibility, he said, to rise to the challenge of this revolution. Change could take place in the world only if *everyone* engaged in the struggle. As he put it, "Whatever affects one directly affects all indirectly. For some strange reason I can never be what I ought to be until you are what you ought to be."

Later in the sermon, King spoke about his role as a civil-rights leader. "There comes a time when one must take the position that it is neither safe nor politic nor popular, but he must do it because conscience tells him it is right."

Dr. King's ultimate achievement was twofold. First, he deeply influenced the politics of his time. But his real victory may have been his ability to follow his conscience — to fight for what he felt was right — against nearly insurmountable odds.

Other books you might enjoy reading

1. Branch, Taylor. *Parting the Waters: America in the King Years, 1954-63.* Simon and Schuster, 1988.

2. King, Coretta Scott. *My Life with Martin Luther King, Jr.* Holt, Rinehart and Winston, 1969.

3. King, Jr., Martin Luther. *Stride Toward Freedom: The Montgomery Story.* Harper & Row, 1958.

4. King, Jr., Martin Luther. *The Trumpet of Conscience.* Harper & Row, 1968.

5. King, Jr., Martin Luther. *Where Do We Go From Here?* Harper & Row, 1967.

6. Oates, Stephen B. *Let the Trumpet Sound: The Life of Martin Luther King Jr.* Harper & Row, 1982.

7. Washington, James M., ed. *A Testament of Hope: The Essential Writings of Martin Luther King Jr.* Harper & Row, 1986.

ABOUT THE AUTHOR

Louise Quayle is the author of several books for young people, among them *Dolphins and Porpoises* (Gallery Books, 1988), *Weather* (Outlet Book Company, 1989), and three books in the *Discover America* series from (W.H. Smith, 1989): *The Backroads of New England, The Sidewalks of New York City,* and *The Backroads of the Pacific Northwest.*